MW00774769

100 DUTCH-LA

From the Medieval Period

to the Present Day

Selected and translated

by

Paul Vincent and John Irons

With an afterword

by

Gaston Franssen

Holland Park Press London

Published by Holland Park Press 2015

Selected by Paul Vincent & John Irons
English translation © Paul Vincent & John Irons 2015

First Edition

A CIP catalogue record for this book is
available from The British Library.

ISBN 978-1-907320-49-1

Cover designed by Reactive Graphics

Printed and bound by CPI Group (UK) Ltd, Croydon, CR0 4YY

www.hollandparkpress.co.uk

100 Dutch-Language Poems – From the Medieval Period to the Present Day is an eclectic selection of poems written in the Dutch language from the 11th century to the present day.

For the poetry lover it is a comprehensive introduction to poetry from the Low Countries and provides a wonderful insight into the themes and issues that influenced generations of poets.

The Dutch language text and the English translations are presented side by side making it a great resource for literature and language students and scholars.

A detailed foreword by Paul Vincent and John Irons who selected and translated the poems, as well as an intriguing afterword by Gaston Franssen, assistant professor of Literary Culture at the University of Amsterdam, add additional value to this necessary anthology.

For Peter King - magistro optimo

With gratitude and affection

LIST OF POEMS

PV – Paul Vincent
JI – John Irons
FJ – Francis Jones

This project was directly inspired by John Irons' successful use of the 100-poem dual-language format in his *100 Danish Poems from the Medieval Period to the Present Day* (Copenhagen/ Seattle, 2011). The germ, however, dates back much further, to our joint encounter with the literature of the Low Countries as undergraduates at Cambridge in the early 1960s, under the inspired tutorship of Peter King. John completed a doctorate on the poet P.C. Boutens and we both went on to teach and translate. (My own field was Dutch language and literature, while John latterly has also translated very widely from the Scandinavian languages in addition to Dutch). However, we like to think we have retained some of the delight and awe of those early years of discovery.

We were both clear that we did not want a scholarly apparatus, apart from a background essay by a university specialist, Gaston Franssen, which highlights the function of landscape in Dutch poetry post 1800.[1] Still, it may be helpful to explain some of our choices as compilers here.

A hundred poems may seem a broad canvas, but that limit has its own constraints. For practical reasons we have restricted the choice to one poem per poet, regardless of our own preferences and established hierarchies. In opting for our own translations throughout (with the sole exception of Francis Jones' virtuoso dialect rendering of Gezelle), we are aware of the gems we are omitting, for example, James S. Holmes' delightful version of 'De leeuw' by De Schoolmeester.

As can be gathered from the opening paragraph, an important selection factor in what is a rare undertaking for Dutch poetry in English translation[2] was personal predilection, deriving from our university study and our reading and teaching since. However, this in itself was not enough. We needed to establish at least a notional canon of 'important' (classic, innovative, influential) works. This was done on the basis of existing anthologies, for the period up to 1990 principally Gerrit

Komrij's epoch-making three-volume *De Nederlandse poëzie* (Bert Bakker, 1980-1994). Needless to say, the idea of 'representativeness' in a work of this modest scope remains a mirage. We are resigned to the fact that readers will lament the absence of some favourites and question the inclusion of other items. In the last analysis these are our personal choices and as such are bound to be partly subjective.

What else besides personal preference influenced our choices? Inevitably, we both had a considerable body of (sometimes published) work in portfolio, but that was not a determining factor, merely convenient when choices coincided. 'Translatability' was also a consideration. As a concept this is fluid and by definition provisional: a poem like Gezelle's ''t Er viel 'ne keer' is only 'untranslatable' until a gifted translator like Francis Jones, who has an affinity with the poem and native-speaker knowledge of a suitable English dialect, brings it to life. Nevertheless, it remains true that not all poems work equally well when transposed into another language. This fact has inevitably affected the process.

'Balance' was another criterion we had to contend with. Perhaps 'balances' would be more appropriate since such pairs are involved as 'earlier/later', 'male/female', 'North/South'. We have been made aware of certain imbalances, for instance, the original absence of women's poetry 1500-1900. This gap has been filled as far as space allowed.

Another important decision was to include the Dutch source texts. This not only increases the teaching value of the book for language and literature students, but by stressing that these are translations rather than original works, an avenue is opened to *translation* criticism and theory. Hopefully, at least some readers will be moved eventually to set aside the translation and tackle the source language itself.

We hope that this selection will prove an accessible introduction to over a millennium of poetry, though we are aware how thankless a task it is to try to find a common denominator in 100 poems spanning such a length of time, the first of them probably scribbled by a Dutch-speaking scribe working in England to test his pen, the last the work of a young, playful, prizewinning twenty-first century female poet. Besides landscape, focused on by Franssen, one might single out a concern with transience and death, a visual, tactile sense and the virtual absence of references to front-line warfare, occupation, heroic patriotism or the nature of poetry. The following schematic survey divides the anthology into ten sections of ten poets each. The numbers can be found in the List of Poems.

Before 1500

As in other Western European medieval literatures, poems 1-10, half of them anonymous, embrace courtly verse (2), epic (3), mysticism (7), didactic poetry (4); secular love lyrics (5,8,10), ballads (6,9).

1500-1700

Poem 11 is a moving first-person defence of female autonomy in relation to men, while the anonymous 12 is set against Anthonis de Roovere's stylish rondeau, 13, a product of the late-medieval Chambers of Rhetoric that thrived in the Low Countries. The Renaissance re-affirms authorial confidence and sees a new openness to foreign models like the sonnet (14,15). Alongside themes of repentance (16), awe at creation (17) and the pain of bereavement, there are evocations of the power of poetry (19,20).

1700-1880

The eighteenth century is represented solely by a haunting image of impermanence (21). A returning exile exults (23); bosom friendship is extolled (22); a lovers' idyll defies the rain (24); 25, a gentle satire, is influenced by English doggerel and nonsense literature, while Holland is praised for its liberal traditions (26), but decried for its appalling climate (27). 28 conjures a pantheist symphony out of a single leaf falling on the water, while 29 is a grimly grotesque view of suicide. 30 is a woman's wry attitude to ageing.

1880-1920

The Movement of 1880 brings an aestheticist agenda and an elegiac tone (31), though 32 testifies to a livelier, enquiring sensibility; 33, 34 and 35 are samples of minimal, introverted nature poetry, while 36 again reflects on transience. 37 uses a traditional rhyming form to express a decidedly modern, disillusioned view of marriage. The author of 38 praises the urban landscape at the expense of the virtually absent countryside of the Netherlands; in 39 death is personified in an almost medieval style. Poem 40 has some hyper-realistic features.

1920-1950

Poem 41, with its resonant sounds, has a nursery-rhyme feel, while 42 takes us back to the Romantic image of the poet as outcast; in 43 the Dutch landscape is remembered from abroad. 44 demonstrates the evocativeness of nonsense, and 45 has a subtle menace. 46 depicts an iconic carillon, while 47 creates a stark word-picture of helplessness; in 48 the poet muses on the nature of simile. 49 is a surreal view of the plant world, giving an original twist to the notion of 'flower power'. One feature worthy of note is the retention of traditional rhyme and metre throughout this modernist period.

1950-1960

The subversive idealism of the Movement of the Fifties is evident in this section in two poetic manifestos, 54 and 56, but there are also more traditional, direct voices expressing bereavement (50) and faithfulness (52); 51 gives a slightly surreal image of war; two poets evoke loss and even oblivion in terms of an empty room (53, 55); in 57 the aftermath of the First World War is simply commemorated, while the visual preoccupation of 58 is clear.

The 1960s

In 59 a child sees her future in a mirror, 60 unemphatically evokes love in an evening landscape in free verse, while 61 reflects on the relationship of body and soul; 62 is an ode to a walnut tree; 63 evokes an ancient monument in the Turkish desert; 64 has a magic, fairy-tale feel; in 65 a poem is compared to a bomb; 66 is a quest for distant safety; in 67 a poet voices his anger; 68 is an appeal to a visual artist to recreate a lost dear one; 69 pokes gentle fun at country life. Poetically it seems a period of 'anything goes.'

The 1970s and 1980

In 70 a river speaks of its own course; in 71 the theme is parental guilt and in 72 atheism. 73 hinges on a child's nosebleed, which triggers intimations of mortality, 74 on an atmospheric old meeting room; 75 brings a Classical myth up to date; 76 describes a rite of passage on the high board; 77 is a children's poem about an old woman, 78 is about the nature of human groups; 79 examines reality and mystery, while 80 is an archaeological view of human history. The concrete tangibility of these poems is striking.

The 1990s

Both 81 and 83 present fish (alive and dead) treated in a playful way; 82 is a female monologue tinged with hysteria; 84 is a contemplative look at a Jewish cemetery; 85 sings the praises of a child's soft skin; in 86 the mad poet Hölderlin is a benign presence. 87 looks back to Hadewijch; 88 could be seen as a companion piece to 47 and 89 is striking for its visual precision. 90 is a light-hearted love song. The level of allusiveness has visibly risen.

2000 and After

In 91 an emotional predicament is given a fairy-tale treatment;

92 invokes Nescio's prose classic 'Little Titans' (1915) in describing the idealism and perplexity of youth and 93 is a variant on the same theme; 94 expresses bewilderment in an extreme landscape; 95 (with which Franssen deals in his afterword) is one of the few explicitly political poems in the anthology; in 96 a burning house is seen as a strange cathartic ritual; 97 chronicles a chance encounter on public transport and an ensuing infatuation; 98 gives loneliness a specific smell and 99 tellingly illustrates the intrusion of the social into private life. Intimacy and 'ordinariness' exist alongside more ambitious themes. Appropriately for the anthology, 100 invokes the 'Big Bang' – in our end is our beginning.

Thanks are due to the following, who have offered help and advice: Ben Bal, Marga de Bolster, Renée Delhez-Van der Wateren, Professor Theo Hermans, Bernadette Jansen op de Haar, Arnold Jansen op de Haar, Thomas Möhlmann and Ronald Spoor. Remaining shortcomings are our own. Finally we should like to thank all copyright-holders who have generously given permission for the original texts to be reprinted here. We are also grateful to Francis Jones for allowing us to include his translation.

Paul Vincent, London & John Irons, Odense
January 2015

1 We would refer readers wanting further information and samples to the following resources:

1)   For general biographical and bibliographical details in Dutch, the digitale bibliotheek voor de Nederlandse letteren (www.dbnl.nl)
2)   The website of Poetry International (poetryinternational web.net), for translated poems and basic information
3)   For background information and cultural and historical contexts for all periods up to 2000, T. Hermans (ed.) *A Literary History of the Low Countries.* Rochester, NY: Camden House, 2009

4)   For a good range of poetry in translation, the annual *The Low Countries*

2 Our only direct competitor in this field, *Dutch Poetry in Translation: Kaleidoscope* by M. Zwart and E. Grene, Wimett, Ill.: Fairfield Books, 1998, is to be commended for the liveliness of its medieval and Renaissance sections. The choice in later periods is very conservative.

100 DUTCH-LANGUAGE POEMS
From the Medieval Period
to the Present Day

HEBBAN OLLA VOGALA NESTAS HAGUNNAN

Hebban olla vogala nestas hagunnan
hinase hic enda thu
wat unbidan we nu

ALL BIRDS ARE A-NESTING

All birds are a-nesting
save me and thee
why now do we tarry

SWER ZE DER MINNE IST SÔ VRUOT

Swer ze der minne ist sô vruot,
    Daz er der minne dienen kan,
Und er durch minne pîne tuot,
    Wol im, derst ein saelic man!
Von minne kumet uns allez guot,
Diu minne machet reinen muot,
    Waz solte ich sunder minne dan?

Ich minne die schoenen sunder danc,
    Ich weiz wol, ir minne ist klâr.
Obe mîne minne ist kranc.
    Sô wirt ouch niemer minne wâr.
Ich sage ir mîner minne danc,
Bî ir minne stât min sanc,
    Er ist tump, swers niht geloubet gar.

WHOE'ER IN LOVE SO WISE CAN BE

Whoe'er in love so wise can be
    That in love's service he'll withstand
The pain from which he'd seek to flee,
    Good luck to him, the happy man!
All goodness we from love get free,
The mind through love gains purity,
    How then should I without love stand?

I love the fair one, will or no,
    And know full well her love is clear.
Should my love have too weak a glow,
    Then no true love can be sincere.
Her for my love I thanks would show,
Without her love my song can't flow,
    Who doubts this is a fool, I fear.

UIT *VAN DEN VOS REYNAERDE*

Willem, die Madocke maecte,
Daer hi dicken omme waecte,
Hem vernoyde so haerde
Dat die avonture van Reynaerde
In Dietsche onghemaket bleven
(Die Aernout niet hevet vulscreven)
Dat hi die vijte dede soucken,
Ende hise na den walschen boeken
In Dietsche dus hevet begonnen.
God moete ons ziere hulpen jonnen! [...]

Het was in eenen tSinxendaghe
Dat beede bosch ende haghe
Met groenen loveren waren bevaen:
Nobel, die coninc, hadde ghedaen
Sijn hof crayeren over al,
Dat hi waende, hadde hijs gheval,
Houden ten wel groeten love.
Doe quamen tes coninx hove
Alle die diere, groet ende cleene,
Sonder vos Reinaert alleene.
Hi hadde te hove so vele mesdaen,
Dat hire niet dorste gaen:
Die hem besculdich kent ontsiet.
Also was Reynaerde ghesciet;
Ende hier omme scuwedi sconinx hof,
Daer hi in hadde cranken lof.
Doe al dat hof versamet was,
Was daer niemen, sonder die das,
Hine hadde te claghene over Reynaerde,
Den fellen metten roden baerde.

FROM *REYNARD THE FOX*

Willem, who did Madoc write,
often till very late at night,
was so disgruntled by the thought
that Reynard's deeds remained unwrought
in our mother tongue to date
(for Aernout found the task too great)
that from French accounts he gleaned
what of Reynard's life he weened
in our language folk might read.
This mighty task we wish godspeed! [...]

Whitsuntide had clothed in green
both shrub and wood, a perfect scene
for King Nobel's summoned court
to which all subjects had to report,
it was, he thought, the perfect chance,
throughout his kingdom to enhance
his glory and his royal fame.
The animals to his court then came
great and small in a single line,
but of Reynard – not a sign.
He'd at court done so much wrong
that he was loath to come along.
He had everything to fear
and his guilt was all too clear,
so he shunned the royal court
where his standing was as nought.
When the assembly was complete
all called Reynard an evil cheat,
except for the badger, and did crave
justice for the red-bearded knave.

UIT DER NATUREN BLOEME

[...]
Daer sijn lieden van andre maniere
ouer ganges die riuiere
dien de lettre hetet bracmanne
van sonderlanghen liue nochtanne
want dats wonderlike dinc
her de gots sone lijf ontfinc
screuen wiselike de gone
vanden vader ende vanden sone
van hare euengheweldechede
an alexandre dor sine bede
ende scinen hare wort openbare
joft kerstinlic gheloue ware
Andre lieden wonen dar neuen
die om te comene in dat leuen
dat na dat steruen comet hier
hem verbernen in .i. vier
ander uolc es daer onuroeder
die haren uader ende hare moeder
alsi van ouden sijn uersleten
te doot slaen ente samen heten
ende dit ouden si ouer weldaet
dies niet ne dade hi hiete quaet
Oec vindemen dar in somech lant
menghen grooten gygant
die .xii. cubitus sijn lanc
ende uolxkin so clene so cranc
cume so groot wi lesent dus
alse .iii. uoeten iofte .ii. cubitus
ar sijn urouwen horic iwagen
die als enewarf kinder draghen
entie werden grau geboren
ende alsi out sijn als wijt horen

28

JACOB VAN MAERLANT c.1230-1240–c.1288-1300

FROM *THE FLOWER OF NATURE*

[...]
There are people of another kind
Past where the Ganges' waters wind.
In histories Brahmin is their name,
With the oddest customs all the same,
For strangely, these folk began,
Before God's son became a man,
To write most sagely of each one,
Of the Father and the Son
And the equal power both possessed
To Alexander at his behest,
And seemed from what their words reveal
To be aflame with Christian zeal.
Near them are other people who,
To reach the long life that will ensue
After down on earth they expire,
Burn themselves upon a fire.
There's also another race of fools
Who when a parent grows old and drools,
When through age his wits grow dim,
Have him killed and feast on him.
They think this is the way to feed,
Those who don't are bad indeed.
Certain countries are the home
Of many mighty giants that roam,
Who are least twelve cubits tall,
Alongside folk who are weedy and small,
Not much taller, the books relate,
Than a cubit or two foot eight.
There are women, I've heard it said,
Who suffer only one childbed.
At birth these females are already grey
And when they're old, or so they say,

29

so werdet hem al grau dat aer
ander wijf wonen dar naer
diere viue bringhen tere drachte
mar sine leuen der iare mar achte
Oec es dar .i. uolc geseten
die die rowe visscen heten
ende drinken die soute ze
ander uolc so wont dar me
die de hande ebben verkert
ende andie voete als men ons lert
ebben si theen twewarf viere
volc esserre van vremder manire
dien de uoeten stan verkert
ende als ons sente ieronimus leert
so esser erande volc vonden.
die sijn gehoeft ghelijc den onden
met crummen clawen ende met langhen
ende met beesten uellen behanghen
ende ouer hare spreken bassen.
[...]

They have completely black hair.
Other women living near there
Who bear five children at one go:
These offspring live only eight years, though.
Another people living near there
Eat raw fish as their main fare
And drink water from the sea
While others in the vicinity
Have hands all placed the wrong way,
And others their feet, so our teachers say:
On each side eight toes for every man.
Then there is a different clan,
Whose feet are not placed where they ought.
As Saint Jerome himself has taught,
People in another place
Were found to have a dog-like face
And both long and crooked claws,
And all dressed in dogskin drawers,
And barked instead of speaking.
[…]

IC SACH NOYT SO RODEN MONT

Ic sach noyt so roden mont
Noch oec so minlike ogen,
Als si heeft, die mi heeft gewont
Al in dat herte dogen.
Doch leve ic in hogen
Ende hope des loen ontfaen:
Geeft si mi qualen dogen
Si mach mis beteren saen.
Lief, mi hevet u minne
So vriendelike bevaen,
Dat ic u met sinne
Moete wesen onderdaen.

Mi es wale, als ic mach sijn
Bi minre scone vrouwen,
Ende is danne haer claer anscijn
Ende haer gelaet mach scouwen.
God verde si van rouwen!
Si es so wale gedaen,
Dat ic haer bi trouwen
Moete tallen diensten staen.
Lief, mi hevet u minne, enz.

I NEVER SAW A MOUTH SO RED

I never saw a mouth so red
Nor eyes of such charm before,
As she has, for whom I've bled
Deep in my heart's core.
Yet my spirits are still high
And I hope for deserving gain:
If she now makes me cry
She can soon cure my pain.
Sweet, my love for you
Has overwhelmed me quite
So I with love so true
Am subject to your might.

All's well with me when I can be
With my beautiful mate
As she shines radiantly
And her face I can contemplate.
God save her from mourning's weight!
She is fairest of all,
So that I must loyally
Be at her beck and call.
Sweet, my love for you, etc.

HEER HALEWIJN

Heer Halewijn zong een liedekijn,
Al die dat hoorde wou bi hem zijn.

En dat vernam een koningskind,
Die was zoo schoon en zoo bemind.

Zi ging voor haren vader staen:
'Och vader, mag ik naer Halewijn gaen?'

'Och neen, gi dochter, neen gi niet!
Die derwaert gaen en keeren niet.'

Zi ging voor hare moeder staen:
'Och moeder, mag ik naer Halewijn gaen?'

'Och neen, gi dochter, neen gi niet!
Die derwaert gaen, en keeren niet.'

Zi ging voor hare zuster staen:
'Och zuster, mag ik naer Halewijn gaen?'

'Och neen, gi zuster, neen gi niet!
Die derwaert gaen en keeren niet.'

Zi ging voor haren broeder staen:
'Och broeder, mag ik naer Halewijn gaen?'

''t Is mi al eens waer dat gi gaet,
Als gi uw eer maer wel bewaert
En gi uw kroon naer rechten draegt.'

Toen is zi op haer kamer gegaen
En deed haer beste kleeren aen.

LORD HALEWIJN

Lord Halewijn sang oh so fine,
All who heard for him did pine.

That was heard by a royal child
So beautiful, beloved, mild.

She spoke unto her father so:
'May I not to Halewijn go?'

'No, my daughter, I must be stern!
Those who go there do not return.'

She spoke unto her mother so:
'May I not to Halewijn go?'

'No, my daughter, I must be stern!
Those who go there do not return.'

She spoke unto her sister so:
'May I not to Halewijn go?'

'Oh no, my sister, I must be stern.
Those who go there do not return.'

She spoke unto her brother so:
'May I now to Halewijn go?'

'I do not care which way you go,
Just mind you guard your honour, though,
And you are worthy of a throne.'

Through her room's door then in she flew,
Her best apparel out she drew.

Wat deed zi aen haere lijve?
Een hemdeken fijnder als zijde.

Wat deed zi aen haer schoon korslijf?
Van gouden banden stond het stijf.

Wat deed zi aen haren rooden rok?
Van steke tot steke een gouden knop.

Wat deed zi aen haren keirle?
Van steke tot steke een peirle.

Wat deed zi aen haer schoon blond hair?
Een krone van goud en die woog zwaer.

Zi ging al in haer vaders stal
En koos daer 't besten ros van al.

Zi zette zich schrijlings op het ros,
Al zingend en klingend reed zi door 't bosch.

Als zi te midden 't bosch mogt zijn,
Daer vond zi mijn heer Halewijn.

Hi bondt sijn peerd aen eenen boom,
De joncvrouw was vol anxt en schroom.

'Gegroet', sei hi, 'gy schoone maegd',
'Gegroet', sei he, 'bruyn oogen clear!'
'Comt, zit hier neer, onbindt u hair.'

Soo menich hair dat si onbondt,
Soo menich traentjen haer ontron.

Zi reden met malkander voort
En op de weg viel menig woord.

And what then did she don at first?
A blouse as fine as a silk purse.

How did she trim her corset fine?
Many gold bands the corset lined.

What things adorned her bright-red frock?
Each stitch had gold buttons like blocks.

What did she wear on her best dress?
At each stitch was a pearl, no less.

What did she put on her blond hair?
A gold crown, so heavy to wear.

She went into her father's stall
And chose the finest mount of all.

She climbed astride her chosen steed,
Sang with joy, and through woods did speed.

Once she had crossed the centre line,
There she met with Lord Halewijn.

He tied his charger to a tree,
The maid felt great anxiety.

'Greetings!' he said, 'my pretty maid',
'Greetings, beauty, those brown eyes there!'
'Come, sit by me, untie your hair.'

As many hairs came from her crown,
As many tears came pouring down.

They rode on further side by side
And much was spoken on their ride.

Zi kwamen al aen een galgenveld;
Daer hing zoo menig vrouwenbeeld.

Alsdan heeft hi tot haer gezeid:
'Mits gi de schoonste maget zijt,
Zoo kiest uw dood! het is noch tijd.'

'Wel, als ik dan hier kiezen zal,
Zoo kieze ik dan het zweerd voor al.

Maer trekt eerst uit uw opperst kleed.
Want maegdenbloed dat spreidt zoo breed,
Zoo 't u bespreide, het ware mi leed.'

Eer dat zijn kleed getogen was,
Zijn hoofd lag voor zyn voeten ras;
Zijn tong nog deze woorden sprak:

'Gaet ginder in het koren
En blaest daer op mynen horen,
Dat al mijn vrienden 't hooren.'

'Al in het koren en gaen ik niet,
Op uwen horen en blaes ik niet.'

'Gaet ginder onder de galge
En haelt daer een pot met zalve
En strijkt dat aen myn rooden hals!'

'Al onder de galge gaen ik niet,
Uw rooden hals en strijk ik niet,
Moordenaers raed en doen ik niet.'

Zi nam het hoofd al bi het haer,
En waschtet in een bronne klaer.

They came upon a gallows field,
Where many women swung and wheeled.

Thereupon to the maid he said:
Since you have quite the fairest head,
Choose your death! For you're not yet dead.'

'Well then, if I'm given the choice,
The sword it is would have my voice.

But first take off your tunic, do,
For blood of virgins splashes too,
I'd hate for it to splash on you.'

Before this action was complete
His head was quickly at his feet.
His tongue, though, managed to entreat:

'Into the cornfield yonder go
And then upon my horn there blow
So that all of my friends may know.'

Into the corn I shall not go,
And on your horn I shall not blow.'

'Go yonder under the gallows
And fetch me a pot of aloes
And rub it on my neck's red rose.'

'Under the gallows I'll not go
Or rub your neck with soft aloe.
I don't heed murderers, you know.'

She picked the head up by its hair
And washed it in a clear spring there.

Zi zette haer schrijlings op het ros,
Al zingend en klingend reed zi door 't bosch.

En als zi was ter halver baen,
Kwam Halewijns moeder daer gegaen:
'Schoon maegd, zaegt gi mijn zoon niet gaen?'

'Uw zoon heer Halewijn is gaen jagen,
G'en ziet hem weer uw levens dagen.

Uw zoon heer Halewijn is dood
Ik heb zijn hoofd in mijnen schoot
Van bloed is mijne voorschoot rood!'

Toen ze aen haers vaders poorte kwam,
Zi blaesde den horen als een man.

En als de vader dit vernam,
't Verheugde hem dat zi weder kwam.

Daer wierd gehouden een banket,
Het hoofd werd op de tafel gezet.

She climbed astride her chosen steed,
Sang with joy, and through woods did speed.

When the journey was halfway done
Halewijn's mother she came upon:
'Fair maiden, have you seen my son?'

'He's hunting, your son Halewijn,
You'll not see him though you may pine.

Your son Lord Halewijn is dead,
And in my lap I have his head,
His blood has made my apron red!'

Reaching her father's gate she blew
On the horn the way that men do.

And when her father heard the sound,
He was glad that she had been found.

Then a great banquet was prepared,
The head with it the table shared.

Dat Suetste Van Minnen Sijn Hare Storme

Dat suetste van minnen sijn hare storme;
Haer diepste afgront es haer scoenste vorme;
In haer verdolen dats na gheraken;
Om haer verhongheren dats voeden ende smaken;
Hare mestroest es seker wesen;
Hare seerste wonden es al ghenesen;
Om hare verdoyen dat es gheduren;
Hare berghen es vinden alle uren;
Om hare quelen dat es ghesonde;
Hare helen openbaert hare conde;
Hare onthouden sijn hare ghichten;
Sonder redenne es hare scoenste dichten;
Hare ghevangnesse es al verloest;
Hare seerste slaen es hare suetste troest;
Hare al beroven es groot vromen;
Hare henen varen es naerre comen;
Hare nederste stille es hare hoechste sanc;
Hare groetste abolghe es hare liefste danc;
Hare groetste dreighen es al trouwe;
Hare droefheit es boete van allen rouwe;
Hare rijcheit es hare al ghebreken.
Noch machmen meer van minnen spreken:
Hare hoechste trouwe doet neder sinken;
Hare hoechste wesen doet diep verdrincken;
Hare grote rijcheit maect armoede;
Haers vele vercreghen toent onspoede;
Hare troesten maect die wonden groot;
Hare hanteren brinct meneghe doet;
Hare voeden es hongher; hare kinnen es dolen;
Verleidinghe es wijse van harer scolen;
Hare hanteren sijn storme wreet;
Hare ghedueren es in onghereet;

LOVE'S SWEETEST IN ITS RAGING STORMS

Love's sweetest in its raging storms;
Its deepest depths are its fairest forms;
While one strays in it, one's goal is near;
To starve for its sake brings nourishing cheer;
Love's despair is knowing for sure;
Its harshest wounds bring their own cure;
Pining for it makes one able to bear;
Hiding it's finding love everywhere;
Dying for it is a salutary pain;
Suppressing it makes its message plain;
What it withholds are its poisoned stings;
Its loveliest poetry wordlessly sings;
Imprisoned in it one finds liberation;
Its cruellest blows are consolation;
Its brings more than it takes by theft;
It comes closer once it has left;
Its deepest silence is soaring song;
It thanks most sweetly when anger's strong;
Its greatest threats are faithful and true;
Its sadness can lessen all our rue;
Its riches are all it does not possess.
Much more can be said of love, I confess:
Its loyal service can drag one down;
Its highest pitch can make one drown;
Its greatest wealth creates poverty;
Winning much love brings adversity;
Its solace makes our wounds grow wide;
By consorting with it so many have died;
Its food is hunger; to know it's to stray;
Its schooling makes us lose our way;
Violent storms are its embrace;
Its fulfilment's just a messy place;

43

Hare toenen es hare selven al helen;
Hare ghichten sijn mere weder stelen;
Hare gheloeften sijn al verleiden;
Hare chierheiden sijn al oncleiden;
Hare waerheit es al bedrieghen;
Hare sekerheyt scijnt meneghen lieghen,
Dies ic ende menich dat orconde
Wel moghen draghen in alre stonde,
Dien de minne dicken hevet ghetoent
Saken daer wij sijn bi ghehoent,
Ende waenden hebben dat hare bleef.
Sint si mi ierst die treken dreef
Ende ic ghemercte al hare seden,
So hildicker mi al anders mede;
Hare ghedreich, hare gheloven
Daer met en werdic meer bedroghen.
Ic wille hare wesen al datse si,
Si goet, si fel: al eens eest mi.

It reveals itself and yet conceals;
The more it gives the more its steals;
Its promises are pure deceit;
Its clothes are nakedness complete;
Its truth misleads us all the while;
Its certainty's often seen as guile,
I and others can make it plain
That this proves true, again and again
We whom love promised prospects fair,
Which turned out to be just empty air,
While we thought love would never fade.
Since love's first tricks on me were played
And I saw through its cunning game
I no longer treated it the same.
However it cajoled and swore
It could not fool me anymore.
As it is, so I too shall be,
Kind or cruel: all's the same to me.

EGIDIUS, WAER BESTU BLEVEN?

Egidius, waer bestu bleven?
Mi lanct na di, gheselle mijn.
Du coors de doot, du liets mi tleven.

Dat was gheselscap goet ende fijn,
Het sceen teen moeste ghestorven sijn.
Nu bestu in den troon verheven
Claerre dan der zonnen schijn,
Alle vruecht es di ghegheven.

Egidius, waer bestu bleven?
Mi lanct na di, gheselle mijn.
Du coors de doot, du liets mi tleven.

Nu bidt vor mi: ic moet noch sneven
Ende in de weerelt liden pijn.
Verware mijn stede di beneven:
Ic moet noch zinghen een liedekijn.
Nochtan moet emmer ghestorven sijn.

Egidius, waer bestu bleven?
Mi lanct na di, gheselle mijn.
Du coors de doot, du liets mi tleven.

46

EGIDIUS, WHERE SHALL I FIND THEE?

Egidius, where shall I find thee?
I long for thee, dear friend of mine.
Thou'st suffered death, to life consigned me.

Sweet company we had and fine,
Yet one must die and the other pine.
Now at the throne mayst thou enshrined be,
There as a brightest sun to shine,
With bliss that's unalloyed assigned thee.

Egidius, where shall I find thee?
I long for thee, dear friend of mine.
Thou'st suffered death, to life consigned me.

Now pray for me: thy death's behind thee,
I to this harsh world must resign.
Keep my place by thee safe, I mind thee:
I still must sing my song's each line.
Yet unto death all lives incline.

Egidius, where shall I find thee?
I long for thee, dear friend of mine.
Thou'st suffered death, to life consigned me.

Het Waren Twee Koninghs Kindren

Het waren twee koninghs kindren,
Sy hadden malkander soo lief;
Sy konden by malkander niet komen,
Het water was veel te diep.

Wat stack sy op drie keerssen,
Drie keerssen van twaelf int pont,
Om daer mee te behouden
's Konincks soone van jaren was jonck.

Met een quam daer een besje,
Een oude fenynde bes,
En die blies uyt de keerssen
Daer verdroncker dien jongen helt.

'Och moeder,' seyde sy, 'moeder,
Mijn hoofje doet mijnder soo wee,
Mocht ik 'er een kort half uurtje
Spanceeren al langhs de zee.'

'Och dochter' seydese, 'dochter!
Alleen en meught ghy niet gaen:
Weckt op u jongste suster,
En laet die met u gaen.'

'Mijn alder jongste suster
Dat is also kleynen kint;
Sy pluckt maer al de roosjes
Die sy in haer wegen vint;

ANON – 14ᵀᴴ CENTURY

There Were Once Two Royal Children

There were once two royal children
Who loved one another so dear;
They could not reach each other,
As the water was deep, I fear.

What did she light? Three candles,
Three candles of twelve to the pound,
To keep for herself the son of the king
Who was young in years and uncrowned.

But along came an old baggage,
An aged and spiteful hag,
And blew out all the candles
Thus drowning the young man.

'O mother,' she said, 'O mother,
My poor head is killing me.
Might I for half an hour
Take a walk along the sea?'

'O daughter,' she said, 'O daughter!
You must not go alone:
Go wake your youngest sister
So you are not on your own.'

'My very youngest sister
Is still a little child;
She just picks all the roses
As she passes a stile;

'Sy pluckt maer al de roosjes,
En die bladertjes laet sy staen,
Dan seggen maer al de lieden,
Dat hebben konincx kinderen gedaen.'

De moeder gingh na de kercke,
De dochter gingh haren gangh:
Zy gingh maer also verre
Daer sy haer vaders visser vant.

'Och visscher,' seydese, 'visscher,
Mijn vaders visscherkijn,
Wout ghy een weynigh visschen,
't Zoud' u wel geloonet zijn.'

Hy smeet sijn net in 't water,
De lootjes gingen te gront,
Hoe haest was daer gevisset
's Koninghs sone van jaren was jonck.

Wat trock sy van haer hande?
Een vingerling root van gout:
'Hout daer myns vaders visser,
Dat isser den loone voor jou.'

Sy nam hem in de armen,
Sy kusten hem voor sijn mont,
'Och mondelingh, kost ghy spreken!
Och hertje waert gy der gesont!'

Zy nam hem in haer armen,
Zy spronker mee in de zee:
'Adieu mijn vader en moeder,
Van u leven siet ghy my niet weer.

She just picks all the roses,
And leaves the leaves behind,
So that all the people say:
Royal children did this, how unkind.'

The mother went to church then,
The daughter did as she wished:
She went so far she found the man
Who caught her father's fish.

'O fisher,' she said, 'O fisher,
My father's fisherman true,
If you will do some fishing
It'll bring profit for you.'

He cast his net in the water,
The leads sank to the sea's ground,
And soon they fished out the king's son
Who was young in years and uncrowned.

What did she take off her hand then?
A ring that was red and gold:
'Take that, my father's fisher,
The reward of which you were told.'

She took him in her arms
And kissed him on the mouth.
'O sweet mouth, if you could speak!
O heart, if you were still sound!'

She took him in her arms
And jumped with him into the sea:
'Adieu, my father and mother,
Never more will you see me.

Adieu mijn vader en moeder,
Mijn vriendekens alle gelijck,
Adieu mijn suster en broeder,
Ick vaerder na 't hemelrijk.'

Adieu, my father and mother
And all you friends of mine,
Adieu my sister and brother,
Now I to heaven will climb.'

GHEQUETST BEN IC VAN BINNEN

Ghequetst ben ic van binnen,
Duerwont mijn hert soe seer,
Van uwer ganscher minnen
Ghequetst soe lanc soe meer.
Waer ic mi wend, waer ik mi keer,
Ic en can gherusten dach noch nachte;
Waer ic mi wend, waer ic mi keer,
Ghi sijt alleen in mijn ghedachte.

MY BREAST IS SORE AFFLICTED

My breast is sore afflicted,
My heart torments me so,
By all thy love inflicted
The wound does ever grow.
Where'er I turn, where'er I go,
By night, by day no rest is given;
Where'er I turn, where'er I go,
By thoughts of thee my heart is riven.

Refereyn

Het es goet vrouwe sijn, maer veel beter heere.
Ghij maegden, ghij weduen, onthoudt dees leere;
Niemandt hem te zeere om houwen en spoede.
Men seydt: daer geen man en es, daer en es geen eere;
Maer die gecrijgen can cost en cleere,
Niet haest haer en keere onder eens mans roede.
Dit es mijnen raedt: weest op u hoede,
Want zoo ic bevroede, ic ziet gemeene,
Als een vrouwe houdt, al esse eel van bloede,
Machtich van goede, zij crijgt aen haer beene
Eenen grooten worpriem; maer blijft zij alleene,
En zij haer reene en zuver gehouden can,
Zij es heere en vrouwe, beeter leven noeyt gheene.
Ic en acht niet cleene thouwelijck, nochtan
Ongebonden best, weeldich wijf sonder man.

Proper meyskens werden wel leelijcke vrouwen,
Arm danten, arm slooren; hoordt jonck metten ouwen!
Dit sou mij doen schouwen thouwelijck voorwaer.
Maer, wachermen, als zij den man eerst trouwen,
Zij meynen de liefde en mach niet vercouwen;
Dan eest hem berouwen eer een half jaer:
Och het pack des houwelijcx es alte zwaer!
Zij wetent claer, diet hebben gedraghen.
Een vrouwe maeckt door vreese menich mesbaer,
Als de man hier en daer gaet druck verjagen,
Drincken en speelen bij nachte, bij dagen;
Dan hoortmen beclagen dat ment oeyt began,
Dan en muegen u helpen vrienden oft magen.
Dus hoordt mijn gewagen en wachter u van:
Ongebonden best, weeldich wijf zonder man.

BALLAD

To be a woman's fine, a man far better.
You maids, you widows keep this to the letter:
Don't haste or fret to see yourselves soon wed.
It's said that manless you are honour's debtor;
If finding food and clothes though does not fetter,
Let no man master both your house and bed.
Take my advice: Be wary where you tread
It seems to me, where'er I cast my gaze,
That if a woman choose – though nobly bred
And rich in goods – to wed she all her days
Will spend short-tethered; if alone she stays
Instead both pure and chaste she'll, I profess,
Be mistress of a life excelling praise.
With marriage I've no quarrel, nonetheless
Not tied by husbands women prosper best.

Maids fair of face make wives plain to behold,
Poor frumps, poor drudges; take care, young and old!
From wedlock's hold I thus should clearly sheer.
Alas, once they are wed they've soon extolled
A love which they believe cannot grow cold;
This they will rue within just half a year:
The yoke of marriage makes life far too drear!
Of this all those who've wed are well aware!
And women make much clamour out of fear
When husbands seek distraction here and there,
Spend nights and days in inn and gambling lair;
Then wives swear that they rue their foolishness,
But friends and family can't ease their care.
So stay on guard, and hear what I profess:
Not tied by husbands women prosper best.

57

Ooc compt de man somtijts droncken en prat,
Als dwijf haer gewracht heeft moede en mat;
Want men moet al wat doen, salmen thuys bestieren.
Wilt zij dan eens rueren haer snatergat,
Zoo werdt sij geslagen med vuysten plat;
Dat droncken vol vat moetse obedieren.
Dan doet hij niet dan kijven en tieren,
Dat sijn de manieren; wee haer diet smaeckt!
Loopt hij dan elders bij Venus camerieren,
Peyst, wat blijder chieren men thuys dan maeckt.
Ghij maegden, ghij vrouwen, aen ander u spaeckt,
Eer ghij ooc gheraeckt in zelcken gespan.
Al waert dat ghij mij al contrarie spraeckt,
Mij en roeckt wiet laeckt, ic blijver weer an:
Ongebonden best, weeldich wijf zonder man.

Eene vrouwe ongehoudt moet derven smans gewin;
Zo en derf zij ooc niet wachten zijnen sin.
En, na mijn bekin, de vrijheydt es veel weerdt.
Zij en werdt niet begresen, gaet sij uut oft in;
En al moest zij leven op haer gespin,
Voorwaer veel te min zij alleen verteerdt.
Een ongebonden vrouwe werdt alom begeerdt,
Al eest datse ontbeerdt eens mans profijt,
Zij es meester en vrouwe aan haren heerdt.
Te gane onverveerdt, dats een groot jolijt.
Zij mach slapen en waken na haren appetijt,
Zonder yemandts verwijt; blijft ongebonden dan,
De vrijheyt te verliezen, geen meerder spijt.
Vroukens, wie ghij sijt, al creegdij eenen goeden Jan,
Ongebonden best, weeldich wijf zonder man.

The man comes home at times drunk as a lord,
Pesters his wife, exhausted by her chores;
No time to pause if she the house shall run.
And should she feel like countering his roars,
He strikes her in the face or to the floor;
That drink-logged vat's commands she may not shun.
For all he'll do is rant and rave at one,
So are things done; poor wife who such must bear!
And if with other women he's begun,
What joy to rule the home when he's not there.
You maids, you women, quench your thirst elsewhere
Ere you would hitch yourself up to distress.
Though you a view opposed to mine all share,
I simply do not care, but still profess:
Not tied by husbands women prosper best.

Unkept, a woman must man's wealth forgo;
His will though likewise she need never know.
And freedom, I maintain, is of great worth.
Without account she's free to come and go;
Though she must spin to earn her bread, all know
To feed one mouth it takes a lesser purse.
Not tied, she's envied everywhere on earth,
And though a husband's income is denied,
As mistress she is master of her hearth.
To freely move is joy none can deride.
To sleep or wake at will she may decide,
With none to chide – so stay untied, don't rest.
Lost freedom is the worst ill ever tried.
Wives everywhere, though good blokes line your nest,
Not tied by husbands women prosper best.

Princesse

Al es een vrouwe noch zo rijck van haven,
Veel mans die achtense als haer slaven.
Ziet toe, alse u laven met schoonen proloogen,
En gelooft niet soo saen, maer laetse draven;
Want mij dunckt, de goey mans sijn witte raven.
Acht niet wat gaven zij u bringen voor oogen;
Alse een vrouwe hebben int nette getoogen,
Es liefde vervloogen, dit sien wij wel.
Int houwen werdt menige vrouwe bedroogen,
Die moeten gedoogen groot zwaer gequel;
Haer goedt werdt verquist, de man valt haer fel.
Ten es vrij geen spel, maer noeyt zwaerder ban.
Tes somtijts om tgeldeken en niet om tvel
Dat de zelcke zoo snel liep dat hij stan.
Ongebonden best, weeldich wijf zonder man.

60

Princess

Though women may have wealth none can deny,
They're viewed as slaves by men both low and high.
Should they with fine words ply, then stop them short
And tell them to push off if they should try;
In number good men with white ravens vie.
Away from all gifts shy that they have brought,
As soon as in their mesh the woman's caught,
Love is as nought, it's seen repeatedly.
In marriage man's deception's grimly taught,
With sorrows fraught, she suffers constantly;
He squanders all her wealth, won't let her be.
No game for free, but heavy curse no less.
Oft money rules not love when you can see
Such men run till their lungs burst out their chest.
Not tied by husbands women prosper best.

HET DAGHET INDEN OOSTEN

'Het daghet inden Oosten,
Het lichtet overal;
Hoe luttel weet mijn liefken
Och waer ick henen sal.'

'Och warent al mijn vrienden
Dat mijn vianden sijn,
Ick voerde u uuten lande,
Mijn lief, mijn minnekijn.'

'Dats waer soudi mi voeren,
Stout ridder wel gemeyt?
Ic ligge in mijns liefs armkens
Met grooter waerdicheyt.'

'Ligdy in uws liefs armen?
Bilo! ghi en segt niet waer.
Gaet henen ter linde groene,
Versleghen so leyt hi daer.'

Tmeysken nam haren mantel
Ende si ghinc enen ganck
Al totter linde groene,
Daer si den dooden vant.

'Och ligdy hier verslaghen,
Versmoort in al u bloet!
Dat heeft gedaen uw roemen
Ende uwen hooghen moet.

The Dawn In The East Is Breaking

'The dawn in the East is breaking.
Light everywhere is found;
Oh how my love knows little
Of where I must be bound.'

'Oh, could they but be friends those
Who now as foes appear,
From this land I would take you,
My love, my darling dear.'

'And where then would you take me,
You knight so bold of face?
In my love's arms I lie in
More virtuous embrace.'

'In your love's arms you're lying?
In faith! No truth you tell.
Seek out the green-leafed linden,
He lies there where he fell.'

The maiden put her cloak on
And to the linden sped,
Where lying on the ground she
Did find her true love dead.

'And is it here you're fallen,
All covered with your blood!
That comes from reckless boasting
And pride that bodes no good.

Och ligdy hier verslaghen
Die mi te troosten plach!
Wat hebdy mi ghelaten
So menighen droeven dach.'

Tmeysken nam haren mantel
Ende si ginck eenen ganck
Al voor haers vaders poorte
Die si ontsloten vant.

'Och is hier eenich heere
Oft eenich edel man,
Die mi mijnen dooden
Begraven helpen can?'

Die heeren sweghen stille,
Si en maecten gheen geluyt;
Dat meysken keerde haer omme,
Si ghinc al weenende uut.

Si nam hem in haren armen
Si custe hem voor den mont
In eender corter wijlen
Tot also menigher stont.

Met sinen blanken swaerde
Dat si die aerde op groef,
Met haer sneewitten armen
Ten grave dat si hem droech.

'Nu wil ic mi gaen begeven
In een cleyn cloosterkijn
Ende draghen swarte wijlen
Ende worden een nonnekijn.'

And is it here you're fallen,
Who solace brought alway!
Now all that you have left me
Is many a mournful day.'

The maiden put her cloak on
And hastened o'er the ground
To where her father's door stood
That she wide open found.

'Oh, is there any squire here
Or some man nobly bred
Who's willing to help bury
my love that now is dead?'

The gentlemen stayed silent,
Of speech they were bereft;
The maiden turned around then,
And shedding tears she left.

Within her arms she held him
And on his mouth did shower
More kisses in a short while
Than in so many an hour.

With his bare sword full-gleaming
The earth she dug away,
With snow-white arms she bore him
And in his grave did lay.

'To some small far-off convent
I now my way will wend,
Henceforth black veils be wearing
And as a nun life end.'

Met hare claerder stemme
Die misse dat si sanck,
Met haer sneewitten handen
Dat si dat belleken clanck.

With voice both clear and ready
The holy mass she sang
With snow-white hands so steady
The little bell she rang.

Rondeel

Die gheen pluymen en can strijcken
Die en dooch ter werelt niet
Is hy aerm, hy en sal niet rijcken
Die gheen pluymen en can strijcken
Alomme soe heeft hy tachterkijcken
Hy wordt verschoven waer men hem siet
Die gheen pluymen en can strijcken
Die en dooch ter wereldt niet.

ANTHONIS DE ROOVERE c.1430–1482

RONDEL

A man who can't fawn and flatter
Is no good upon this earth
For he will stay poor no matter
A man who can't fawn and flatter
Will see his ambitions shatter
He's sidelined and has no worth
A man who can't fawn and flatter
Is no good upon this earth.

SONET

Isser iemant onder des hemels ronde
Die gheproeft heeft Cupidos tyrannie,
Dat ben ick wel, die met herten onblye
Ghequetst ben met een dootelycke wonde
Die hy my ghaf door d'ooghe van de blonde,
Stellende heur soo in de heerschappye
Ouer myn hert en sinnen t'allen tye,
Beruerende myn siele tot den gronde.
Nacht ende dach en doen ick niet dan claghen,
Suchten, kermen, ende myn herte cnaghen,
Biddende hem dat hy myn leuen eynde.
Maer laes hy neempt in myn smerte behaghen,
Want hoe ick hem roepe en smeeke by vlaghen,
Hy en vertroost my niet waer ick my weynde.

JAN VAN DER NOOT c.1539–after 1595

SONNET

If anyone under the arc of the sky
Has tasted Cupid's tyrannous dart,
It's I, who with a heart torn apart,
Have been sorely wounded and now must die.
He pierced me, through the blonde one's eye,
Making her mistress of all my heart
And of my senses, till death do us part,
And making my soul in agony cry.
Day and night I can only complain
And sigh and fret and groan again,
Beseeching him to end my days,
But alas, he takes pleasure in my pain,
For however I call and beg and explain,
He brings no relief to my tear-filled gaze.

GESWINDE GRIJSAERT

Geswinde grijsaert die op wackre wiecken staech,
De dunne lucht doorsnijt, en sonder seil te strijcken,
Altijdt vaert voor de windt, en ijder nae laet kijcken,
Doodtvyandt van de rust, die woelt bij nacht bij daech;
Onachterhaelbre Tijdt, wiens heten honger graech
Verslockt, verslint, verteert al watter sterck mach lijcken
En keert, en wendt, en stort Staeten en Coninckrijcken;
Voor ijder een te snel, hoe valtdij mij soo traech?
Mijn lief sint ick u mis, verdrijve' jck met mishaeghen
De schoorvoetighe Tijdt, en tob de lange daeghen
Met arbeidt avontwaerts; uw afzijn valt te bang.
En mijn verlangen can den Tijdt god niet beweghen.
Maer 't schijnt verlangen daer sijn naem af heeft gecreghen,
Dat jck den Tijdt, die jck vercorten wil, verlang.

FAST-FLYING ANCIENT

Fast-flying ancient who, winging your tireless way,
Cleaving ethereal air, full-sailed and onward speeding,
Always before the wind, leave us behind, unheeding,
Arch-enemy of rest, who storms on night and day;
Time, who outrun us all, who, ravenous, hold sway,
Devour and consume, on those who seem strong feeding,
Toying with realms at will, states to their downfall leading;
Too swift for all the world, why do you now delay?
My love, since you're not here, I while, with restless nagging,
The sluggish time away, toil on when days are dragging,
And labour towards eve; with you gone, I'm distraught.
My longing is acute, and still the Time God tarries.
But longing seems to take the very name it carries
From making time grow long, when I would cut it short.

GEESTIGH LIEDT
Stem: Ick schou de Wereld an

Wat dat de wereld is,
Dat weet ick al te wis
(God betert) door 't versoecken:
Want ick heb daer verkeert
En meer van haer geleerd
Als vande beste boecken.

Want of ick schoon al las
Het geen soo kunstich was
Als Goddelijck geschreven,
Ten gingh ter ziel noch sin
Soo nyver my niet in
Als 't eygen selfs beleven.

Nu heb ick 't al versocht:
Soo dool, als onbedocht,
Soo rauw als onberaden.
Och Godt! ick heb te blind
En al te seer bemind
De dingen die my schaden.

Een hooft vol wind en wijn,
Een hart vol suchts en pijn,
Een lichaem gants vol qualen
Heeft Venus en de kroes,
Of selfs die leyde droes,
My dickwils doen behalen

GERBRAND ADRIAENSZ. BREDERO 1585–1618

DEVOUT SONG
Melody: Ick schou de Wereld an by Petrus Dathenus

What the world has to tell,
I know it all too well
(Oh God) from experience:
I've spent time in company,
Learned more from living free
Than from books and documents.

For study as I might
Things full of art and quite
Divine in inspiration;
They did not penetrate
My heart or senses' gate
Like my first-hand sensation.

I've tried all I could find:
With mad, impetuous mind
Both crudely and thoughtlessly.
Oh God, I blindly chased,
Devotedly embraced
The things that injure me.

Head full of wind and wine,
Heart that sighs as I pine,
A body in agony
That Venus and the cup,
Passion that churns me up,
Too often inflict on me.

Och! een bedroeft gemoet
En een hert seer verwoet
Van duysent na berouwen
Van overdaet en lust,
Met een ziel ongerust
Heb ick in 't lest behouwen.

Hoe strengh breeckt my dit op:
Myn kruijfde krulde kop
Die brenght mijn voor de jaren,
In mijn tijds Lenten voort,
Op 't swart en 't swetigh swoort
Veel grijse graeuwe hayren.

Wanneer een ander leyt
Gestreckt en uytgespreyt
En rust met lijf en leden:
Dan plaeght my aldermeest
De quellingh van mijn Geest
Met beulsche wredicheden.

Dan dringht my door de huyt
Het bange water uyt,
Door kommerlijcke sorgen,
Dies my het herte barst
En wenscht alsoo gheparst
Den ongeboren morgen.

En nimmer ick den dagh
Alsoo geluckich sagh,
Dat sy my vol verblyden:
Voorwaer 't heb uur noch tijd,
Of ellick heeft syn strijd,
Sijn lief, zijn leed, zijn lyden.

Oh, a mind that grief has cracked
A heart that's sorely racked
By thousandfold contrition,
By rank lecherousness,
A soul that knows just stress –
This is now my condition.

How harsh the cost I bear:
My black and curly hair
Brings me before my time,
While I'm in the prime of life –
On my sweaty pate they're rife –
Many locks that are grey as rime.

While others take their ease,
Lie sprawled out as they please
And rest their weary frames,
That's when my tortured soul
Plagues me and takes its toll
With horrid hellish flames.

The sweat pours from its source
Through skin now finds its course,
Driven by care and mourning,
So my heart seems to break
And longs, while at the stake,
For day that's not yet dawning.

 I never saw the day
That was itself so gay
It cheered me till the morrow:
Not an hour of my life
That lacks its share of strife,
Its love, its grief, its sorrow

Al 't gene dat de Lie'n
Ter Wereld mogen sien
Of immermeer verwerven,
En wensch ick niet soo seer
Als saligh inden Heer
Te leven en te sterven.

All that we humans may
See in the world's display;
Or ever may acquire,
I don't want such reward
But blissful with the Lord
To live and then expire.

Scheppinge

God heeft de werelt door onsichtbare clavieren
Betrocken als een luyt met al sijn toebehoor.
Den hemel is de bocht vol reyen door en door,
Het roosken, son en maen die om ons hene swieren.

Twee grove bassen die staech bulderen en tieren
Sijn d'aerd' en d'oceaan: de quinte die het oor
Verheuget, is de locht: de reste die den choor
Volmaket, is t'geboomt en allerhande dieren.

Dees luyte sloech de Heer met sijn geleerde vingers,
De engels stemden in als treffelicke singers,
De bergen hoorden toe, de vloeden stonden stil:
Den mensch alleen en hoort noch sangeren noch snaren,
Behalven dien 't de Heer belieft te openbaren
Na zijn bescheyden raet en Goddelijcken wil.

CREATION

God with his wires invisible has strung the world
As 'twere a lute, with all of its accoutrements.
The welkin is the bowl, full-ribbed from end to end,
The rose, the sun and moon whose orbits round us twirl.

The two coarse bass strings that forever boom and roar
Are earth and ocean: the high chanterelle, so sweet
Upon the ear, the sky: the others that complete
The choir are the trees and beasts of every sort.

This lute th'Almighty plucked with His accomplished fingers,
The angels then joined in as His proficient singers,
The mountains listened rapt, the rivers all stood still:
And man alone hears neither singers nor the strings,
Unless it pleases God to reveal to him such things
According to His prudent plan and heav'nly will.

Uitvaert Van Mijn Dochterken

De felle Doot, die nu geen wit magh zien,
Verschoont de grijze liên.
Zij zit omhoogh, en mickt met haren schicht
Op het onnozel wicht,
En lacht, wanneer, in 't scheien,
De droeve moeders schreien.
Zij zagh 'er een, dat wuft en onbestuurt,
De vreught was van de buurt,
En, vlugh te voet, in 't slingertouwtje sprong;
Of zoet Fiane zong
En huppelde, in het reitje
Om 't lieve lodderaitje:
Of dreef, gevolght van eenen wackren troep,
Den rinckelenden hoep
De straten door: of schaterde op een schop:
Of speelde mct de pop,
Het voorspel van de dagen,
Die d'eerste vreught verjagen:
Of onderhiel, met bickel en boncket
De kinderlijcke wet,
En rolde en greep, op 't springend elpenbeen
De beentjes van den steen;
En had dat zoete leven
Om geldt noch goet gegeven:
Maar wat gebeurt? terwijl het zich vermaackt
Zoo wort het hart geraackt,
(Dat speelzieck hart) van eenen scharpen flits,
Te dootlick en te bits.
De Doot quam op de lippen
En 't zieltje zelf ging glippen
Toen stont helaas! de jammerende schaar
Met tranen om de baar,
En kermde noch op 't lijck van haar gespeel,

82

MY YOUNG DAUGHTER'S FUNERAL

Ferocious Death that hates what's pure and fair
Spares old folk with grey hair.
It sits on high and aims its shaft of spite
At the poor guiltless mite,
And laughs when, at her dying,
Sad mothers are all crying.
One girl it spied was, in her headstrong flight,
The neighbourhood's delight,
She skipped with ropes on nimble feet,
Or sang a song so sweet,
And with her friends in a row
Tripped to see a puppet show;
Or, racing ahead of her gallant troop,
Drove on the loudly ringing hoop
All through the streets; or else laughed aloud on swings;
Or played with dolls and things:
A prelude to later years,
When first joy disappears;
Or she obeyed, with marbles and with taws,
Childhood's own severe laws,
And rolled and grabbed, as the ivory flew,
The knucklebones up anew;
And thought her life so handsome,
Worth more than a king's ransom.
But what occurs? While she is at her play,
Her little heart falls prey
(Her playful heart) to a sharp lightning flash
That fells her with its lash.
Then Death rose to her lip,
And made her poor soul slip
Away. The host of mourners wailed out loud,
Round the coffin, heads bowed.
They groaned to see their little comrade's fate,

En wenschte lot en deel
Te hebben met haar kaartje,
En doot te zijn als *Saertje*
De speelnoot vlocht (toen 't anders niet moght zijn)
Een krans van roosmarijn
Ter liefde van heur beste kameraat
O krancke troost! wat baat
De groene en goude loover?
Die staatsi gaat haast over.

Wished they could join her straight
There upon the solemn bier
And die like young *Sara* here.
A playmate wove (after all hope had gone)
A wreath with rosemary on,
Expressing love for her best childhood friend.
Vain solace! To what end
Are green-gold leaves displayed?
Their pomp will quickly fade.

AEN MIJN HEER HOOFT
OP HET OOVERLYDEN VAN MEVROUW VAN SULECOM.

Die als een Baeck in zee van droefheidt wort gehouwen
Geknot van stam en tack, en echter leeven moet,
Zeijnt uw dit swack behulp voor 't troosteloos gemoet,
Gedompelt in een meer Van Baerelijcke rouwen.
Zeght *Vastaert* dat hij moght pampieren raet vertrouwen
Zoo dinnerlycke smart zich schriftlyck uyten kon,
Hij staroogh in liefs glans als Aedlaer in de Son,
En stel sijn leed te boeck, zoo heeft hij 't niet t'onthouwen.
Pampier was 't waepentuijch waermee ick heb geweert
Te willen sterven, eer 't den Heemel had begeert,
Daer ooverwon ick mee, en deed mijn Vijand wycken,
Zijn eijgen lesse leer hem matijghen zyn pijn,
Want quelling op de maat en kan soo fel niet sijn.
Besweer hem dat hij sing op maetsangh droevelijcken.

MARIA TESSELSCHADE ROEMERS VISSCHER
1594–1649

To my Lord Hooft
on the death of my Lady of Zuilichem (wife of Constantijn Huygens)

One like a beacon set midst seas of lamentation
With trunk and branch cut off, who ways to live must find,
Sends this poor relief to a disconsolate mind,
Submerged within a lake by waves of aggravation.
Tell *Constant* he could find some paper consolation
If his internal pain in writing he could share.
Let him stare at love's sun, like eagles brave its glare,
His grief in print express: no need for conservation.
Paper was the weapon I used to keep at bay
The urge to die before the Heavens' appointed day.
I overcame my grief, routed my foe at leisure.
Let his own lesson teach him how to lessen pain,
Since grief in measured rhyme is surely less a bane.
Entreat him then to sing in stately, mournful measure.

DICHTENS KRACHT

Wie heeft het Dicht verdicht? Ick kan den Mann niet prijsen.
Wat's Voet-maet, en wat's Rijm in d'ooren vande wijsen?
Is 't wijsheit diemen spreeckt? die luydt wel ongerijmt.
Is 't jock en mallicheit? wat lightm'er mé en lijmt.
En spilt syn' dieren tijd, en pijnight syn' gedachten,
Om Rijmen, die veeltijds de Reden maer verkrachten?
Dit's waerheit: en nochtans een eertyds wijse Mann
Prees 'tdichten wijsselick, en gaf'er reden van:
De woorden, zei die wijs', en zyn niet te verachten,
Die doorden wreeden drang van eng-geboorde Schachten
Haer selven uijteren: sij waeren daer geknelt,
En brekender scherp uijt, geslepen met geweld,
En byten ons in 'toor. En dit is vast te setten,
Als blasen inde Locht en blasen door Trompetten,
Soo scheelt het Dichteloos te spreken en in Dicht.
Ick laet een yeder een 'tscheel deelen soo het light.

CONSTANTIJN HUYGENS 1596–1687

POETRY'S POWER

What man invented verse? His efforts I can't prize.
What's Metre and what's Rhyme when heard by those who're wise?
Is wisdom spoken thus? There seems no sense or rhyme.
Mere jest and silliness? Why while away one's time,
And waste one's precious hours and rack one's brains till late
On Rhymes which frequently appear to violate
Our Reason? Still, a Sage who lived in times gone by
Praised poems in wise terms, and then informed us why.
The words, maintained the sage, we cannot just ignore,
Which, once they have been squeezed into a narrow Bore,
Express themselves aloud: at first tightly confined,
They now burst sharply out, and by the force refined,
Strike hard upon our ears. And this we can notate
Like breath blown into Air or sounds Fanfares create.
Thus Poetry stands apart from Prose in human speech.
I'll make the difference clear, permit me, to you each.

AIR

Droom is 't leven, anders niet;
't Glijdt voorby gelijk een vliet,
Die langs steyle boorden schiet,
Zonder ooyt te keeren.
D'Arme mensch vergaapt sijn tijt,
Aan het schoon der ydelheyd,
Maar een schaduw die hem vlijt,
Droevig! wie kan 't weeren?
D'Oude grijse blijft een kint,
Altijd slaap'rig, altijd blind;
Dag en uure,
Waard, en duure,
Wordt verguygelt in de wind;
Daar me glijdt het leven heen,
't Huys van vel, en vlees, en been,
Slaat aan 't kraaken,
d'Oogen waaken,
Met de dood in duysterheen.

AIR

Life is nothing but a dream,
Gliding past us like a stream,
Between steep banks its flow can seem
Like a never-turning tide.
Poor humans gawp away their days
At vain beauty in a haze,
Just a flattering shadow that plays.
So sad! Which of us can stop the slide?
The greybeard has an infant's mind,
Always sleepy, always blind.
Days and hours,
Memory's powers,
The winds just juggle and wind,
And so life can vanish on its own,
The house of skin and flesh and bone
Starts to break,
The Eyes stay awake
With death in the dark alone.

De Zielsvriendin

De ziel van onze ziel, de geest van onzen geest,
De leidsvrouwe onzer jeugd, het leeven van ons leeven;
Een artseny, die ziels- en ligchaams-kwaal geneest;
Een rykdom, die ons meer dan hy bezit kan geeven;
Een trouwe raadster, in het allerhaglykst uur;
Een teedre troosteres in 't felst der tegenspoeden;
Een schenkster van het zoet, een deelster in het zuur;
Een vyandin van kwaad, van liefdeloos vermoeden;
Een dierbre wederhelft, een trouwe lotgenoot,
Een schat waarom men nooit te veel, te lang, kan delven;
Een voedsel voor de ziel, een zuiver geestlyk brood,
Een ander-ik en een waarächtig eigenzelven;
Een teder oog dat op den grond van 't harte ziet;
Een hand die, als zy slaat, nooit slaat dan om te heelen;
Een ziel die alles derft, zo 't lichaam niets geniet,
En alles smaakt, mag zy haar 't ligchaam mededeelen;
Het allerwaardigst goed dat ooit een stervling vindt,
Nooit aftebeelden door de leevendigste trekken;
Een band, die d'aardworm aan zyn eeuwige Oorzaak bindt:
Dit zal de beeldtnis van een Zielsvriendin verstrekken.

THE SOULMATE

The spirit of our spirit, soul within our soul,
The one who guides our youth, the life that we are living,
A remedy to make our soul and body whole;
A wealth whose bounty grows the more that it is giving;
A steadfast counsellor in our most threatening hour,
A tender solacer of life's worst dispensation,
A bearer of what's sweet, she shares when things turn sour,
An enemy of bad and loveless speculation;
A precious other half, a true friend till one's dead,
A treasure one can't dig or toil enough in freeing,
A soul's best sustenance, the spirit's purest bread,
A second self and yet a fully separate being;
A tender eye that sees the heart's most inward core;
A hand that never strikes unless to bring one healing.
A soul that all things spurns which fleshly joys ignore,
And all will taste if she can share them with true feeling;
Most precious thing of all a mortal ever finds,
Which cannot be described by the most vivid phrases;
Link which the earthworm to its Cause Eternal binds:
Such images as these can sing a soulmate's praises.

Aan Den Hollandschen Wal

'k Heb dan met mijn strammen voet,
Eindlijk uit d'onstuimen vloed,
Hollands vasten wal betreden!
'k Heb mijn kromgesloofde leden
Op zijn bodem uitgestrekt;
'k Heb hem met mijn lijf bedekt;
'k Heb hem met mijn arm omvademd;
'k Heb zijn lucht weêr ingeademd;
'k Heb zijn hemel weêrgezien,
God geprezen op mijn kniên,
Al de doorgestane smarte
Weggebannen uit mijn harte,
En het graf van mijn geslacht,
Dit mijn rif teruggebracht! –

'k Hcb dit, en, genadig God!
Hier voleinde ik thands mijn lot!
Laat, na zoo veeljarig sterven,
Mij dat einde thans verwerven!
Dit, ô, God, is al mijn hoop
Na zoo wreed een levensloop!

WILLEM BILDERDIJK 1756–1831

ON HOLLAND'S SHORE

So, with stiff feet at last I've stepped
From the flood that round me swept
Onto Holland's solid shore!
My limbs, more toil-worn than before,
I've stretched out on its earth,
Covered it with my poor girth;
I've embraced it with my arm,
Inhaled once more its air's sweet charm.
I've seen its sky again, and trees
And praised the Lord upon my knees.
All the pain that's made me smart
Has been banished from my heart,
And to the tomb of my own line
I've brought back these poor limbs of mine! –

Oh Gracious God, all this I've done!
Here I'll die when life's course is run!
After long years of lingering death,
Let me here draw my final breath!
This hope, my God, is enough for me
After so cruel a destiny!

HERDENKING

Wij schuilden onder dropplend lover,
Gedoken aan den plas;
De zwaluw glipte 't weivlak over,
En speelde om 't zilvren gras;
Een koeltjen blies, met geur belaân,
Het leven door de wilgenblaân.

't Werd stiller; 't groen liet af van droppen;
Geen vogel zwierf meer om;
De daauw trok langs de heuveltoppen,
Waar achter 't westen glom;
Daar zong de Mei zijn avendlied!
Wij hoorden 't, en wij spraken niet.

Ik zag haar aan, en diep bewogen,
Smolt ziel met ziel in een.
O tooverblik dier minlijke oogen,
Wier flonkring op mij scheen!
O zoet gelispel van dien mond,
Wiens adem de eerste kust verslond!

Ons dekte vreedzaam wilgenloover;
De scheemring was voorbij;
Het duister toog de velden over;
En dralend rezen wij.
Leef lang in blij herdenken voor,
Gewijde stond! geheiligd oord!

A.C.W. STARING 1767–1840

REMEMBRANCE

We sheltered under dripping willows,
Hunched at the waterside;
The swallow slipped across the meadows,
And over the sleek grass plied;
A cooling breeze brim-full of scent
Roused the willows as it went.

It grew quiet; leaves shed no more raindrops;
No more birds roamed about;
The dew moved across the hilltops,
Beyond which the sunset shone out;
Then May sang forth its evening air!
We heard it and were silent there.

I saw her face and, with great emotion,
Our souls merged into one.
Her eyes, enchanting, caused a commotion,
Their glow shone like the sun!
The lisping of her mouth was sweet,
She swallowed my first kiss complete!

Our bed of peaceful leaves of willow;
Dusk gave way to night's throes;
Darkness moved across each meadow;
We two, lingering, rose.
Live long in joyful memory,
Hallowed hour, sanctuary!

De Aap

Een aap,
Schoon kleiner dan een schaap,
Is echter een veel verstandiger knaap,
En zou zich zoo gemaakelijk niet laten scheren,
Als een schaap doet, in zijn wollen kleêren.

Een aap is zeer amusant,
Vooral in zijn geboorteland,
En heeft in zijn jeugd veel grappiger manieren
Dan de meeste jongeluî onder de dieren.
Het klimmen en klauteren doet hy net zo vlug als een kat,
En hy rijdt te paard op een hond, als iemand die er les in
    heeft gehad.
Van amandelen houdt hy veel en van nooten,
En wat een ander met zijn handen zou doen, doet hy met
    zijn pooten.
Daar is altijd groot dispuut geweest
Of een aap eigentlijk een mensch is of een beest;
En dat verwondert ons ook niet,
Daar men zoveel apen onder de menschen ziet.

THE APE

Apes,
Though puny jackanapes,
Are too smart by far for serious scrapes,
And would not be shorn so easily
As a sheep clothed in wool can be.

An ape's an amusing beast,
In its native land at least,
And its youth has funnier habits
Than other young, including rabbits.
In climbing and clambering it's as nimble as a cat,
And it rides astride a dog as if it had learnt it off pat.
It adores almonds and other nuts to eat,
And what others would do with their hands, it does with
    its feet.
People have long hotly disagreed
Whether an ape is beast or man, indeed;
And that does not surprise us, mind,
Since so many apes are found among mankind.

HOLLAND

Grauw is uw hemel en stormig uw strand,
Naakt zijn uw duinen en effen uw velden,
U schiep natuur met een stiefmoeders hand,
Toch heb ik innig u lief, o mijn Land!

Al wat gij zijt, is der Vaderen werk;
Uit een moeras wrocht de vlijt van die helden,
Beide de zee en den dwing'land te sterk,
Vrijheid een tempel en Godsvrucht een kerk.

Blijf, wat gij waart, toen ge blonkt als een bloem;
Zorg, dat Europa den zetel der orde,
Dat de verdrukte zijn wijkplaats u noem',
Land mijner Vad'ren, mijn lust en mijn roem!

En wat de donkere toekomst bewaart,
Wat uit haar zwangere wolken ook worde,
Lauw'ren behooren aan 't vleklooze zwaard,
Land, eens het vrijst en gezegendst der aard.

E.J. POTGIETER 1808–1875

HOLLAND

Grey are your heavens and stormy your strand,
Bare are your dunes and dead-flat your acres,
Nature employed here a stepmother's hand,
Yet I love you dearly, my own native Land!

All that you are our forefathers have made;
From a morass the toil of those makers,
Who resisted both sea and tyranny's blade,
Built a temple to Freedom and true Faith displayed.

Stay as you were when you shone like a flower;
Ensure Europe calls you true order's shrine,
The refuge of those oppressed by harsh power,
Land of my Race, my joyous, safe bower!

Whatever dark future we now look toward
Whatever pregnant storm clouds design,
Laurels befit the immaculate sword.
Land, once the freest, most blest by the Lord.

BOUTADE

O land van mest en mist, van vuilen, kouden regen,
Doorsijperd stukske grond, vol killen dauw en damp,
Vol vuns, onpeilbaar slijk en ondoorwaadbre wegen,
Vol jicht en parapluies, vol kiespijn en vol kramp!

O saaie brij-moeras, o erf van overschoenen,
Van kikkers, baggerlui, schoenlappers, moddergoôn,
Van eenden groot en klein, in allerlei fatsoenen,
Ontvang het najaarswee van uw verkouden zoon!

Uw kliemerig klimaat maakt mij het bloed in de aderen
Tot modder; 'k heb geen lied, geen honger, vreugd noch
      vreê.
Trek overschoenen aan, gewijde grond der Vaderen,
Gij – niet op mijn verzoek – ontwoekerd aan de zee.

BOUTADE

Oh land of filth and fog, of vile rain chill and stinging,
A sodden fetid plot of vapours dank and damp,
A vast expanse of mire and blocked roads clogged and
    clinging,
Brimful of gamps and gout, of toothache and of cramp!

Oh dreary mushy swamp, oh farmyard of galoshes,
With marsh frogs, dredgers, cobblers, mud gods overrun,
With every shape and size of duck that therein sploshes,
Receive this autumn dirge from your besnotted son!

To mud your claggy climate makes my blood set slowly;
Song, hunger, joy and peace are all withheld from me.
Pull your galoshes on, ancestral ground most holy,
You – not at my request – once wrested from the sea.

'T Er Viel 'Ne Keer

(Herinnering aan Beethovens Septuor)

't Er viel 'ne keer een bladtjen op
    het water
't Er lag 'ne keer een bladtjen op
    het water
En vloeien op het bladtje dei
    dat water
En vloeien dei het bladtjen op
    het water
En wentelen winkelwentelen
    in 't water
Want 't bladtje was geworden lijk
    het water
Zoo plooibaar en zoo vloeibaar als
    het water
Zoo lijzig en zoo leutig als
    het water
Zoo rap was 't en gezwindig als
    het water
Zoo rompelend en zoo rimpelend
    als water
Zoo lag 't gevallen bladtjen op
    het water
En m' ha' gezeid het bladtjen ende
    'et water
't En was niet 't een een bladtje en 't an-
    der water
Maar water was het bladtje en 't blad-
    tje water
En 't viel ne keer een bladtjen op
    het water

A LITTLE LEAF ONCE FLUTTERED ...

(Remembering Beethoven's Septet)

A little leaf once fluttered down
    to t' watter
A little leaf once floated down
    to t' watter
And flowing onto t' little leaf
    cam' t' watter
And it were flowing, t' little leaf,
    on t' watter
And theer it twirled and swirled about
    i' t' watter
For now that leaf were well-nigh t' same
    as watter
And theer it mickle-trickled just
    like watter
And theer it dandle-dawdled just
    like watter
And theer it skittle-scuttled just
    like watter
And theer it ripple-ruffled just
    like watter
That little ligging fallen leaf
    on t' watter
Until tha could ha' said that t' leaf
    and t' watter
Weren't one of 'em a leaf and t' oth-
    er watter
But t' watter now were leaf, and t' leaf
    were watter
A little leaf once fluttered down
    to t' watter

Als 't water liep het bladtje liep.
   Als 't water
Bleef staan, het bladtje stond daar op
   het water
En rees het water 't bladtje rees
   en 't water
En daalde niet of 't bladtje daalde
   en 't water
En dei niet of het bladtje dei't
   in 't water
Zoo viel der eens een bladtjen op
   het water
En blauw was 't aan den Hemel end'
   in 't water
En blauw en blank en groene blonk
   het water
En 't bladtje loech en lachen dei
   het water
Maar 't bladtje en wa' geen bladtje neen
   en 't water
En was nie' méér als 't bladtjen ook
   geen water
Mijn ziele was dat bladtjen: en
   dat water? –
Het klinken van twee harpen wa'
   dat water
En blinkend in de blauwte en in
   dat water
Zoo lag ik in den Hemel van
   dat water
Den blauwen blijden Hemel van
   dat water!
En 't viel ne keer een bladtjen op
   het water
En 't lag ne keer een bladtjen op
   het water.

When t' watter flowed, t' leaf flowed and all.
 When t' watter
Were still, then t' leaf lay just as still
 on t' watter
When t' watter rose, t' leaf rose along
 wi' t' watter
When t' watter fell, t' leaf fell as sharp
 as t' watter
What t' watter did, t' leaf did and all
 i' t' watter
This leaf it fluttered any road
 to t' watter
And t' sky were blue and it were blue
 i' t' watter
One glistening gleam o' blue and green
 were t' watter
And t' leaf it laughed and wi' it laughed
 all t' watter
But t' leaf it weren't no leaf now, it
 were watter
And it were nobbut leaf, were all
 that watter
That little leaf, it were my soul:
 and t' watter? –
A ringing o' two harps it were,
 that watter
And glist'ning i' that gleaming blue
 o' t' watter
I lay in Heaven in a sky
 o' watter
In Heaven's blissful blue in all
 that watter
A little leaf once fluttered down
 to t' watter
A little leaf once floated down
 to t' watter.

De Zelfmoordenaar

In het diepst van het woud
  – 't Was al herfst en erg koud –
Liep een heer in zijn eentje te dwalen.
Och, zijn oog zag zoo dof!
En zijn goed zat zoo slof!
En hij tandknerste, als was hij aan 't malen.

'Ha!' dus riep hij verwoed,
''k Heb een adder gebroed,
Neen, erger, een draak aan mijn borst hier!'
En hij sloeg op zijn jas,
En hij trapte in een plas;
't Spattend slik had zijn boordjes bemorst schier.

En meteen zocht zijn blik
Naar een eiketak, dik
Genoeg om zijn lichaam te torschen,
Daarnaa haalde hij een strop
Uit zijn zak, hing zich op.
En toen kon hij zich niet meer bemorsen.

Het werd stil in het woud
En wel tienmaal zoo koud,
Want de wintertijd kwam. En intusschen
Hing maar steeds aan zijn tak,
Op zijn doode gemak,
Die mijnheer, tot verbazing der musschen.

PIET PAALTJENS 1835–1894

The Suicide

Where deep woods enfold
– It was autumn and cold –
A solitary gent came a-winding.
Oh, so dim was his eye!
And his clothes were awry!
And he grated his teeth as if grinding.

'Ha,' in fury he said,
'A vile serpent I've bred,
Worse, a dragon deep in my breast here!'
And his own coat he struck,
In a puddle got stuck,
While the mud nigh spattered his best gear.

And at once he looked round
For a thick oak branch, sound
Enough to support his whole body.
Then he took out a rope
From his pocket, lost hope,
And could no longer spill and look shoddy.

It turned quiet in the trees
And it started to freeze,
As the wintertime came with its arrows,
While he hung from his tree,
Just as cool as could be,
That poor gent, and astonished the sparrows.

En de winter vlood heen,
Want de lente verscheen,
Om opnieuw voor den zomer te wijken.
Toen dan zwierf – 't was erg warm –
Er een paar arm in arm
Door het woud. Maar wat stond dát te kijken!

Want, terwijl het, zoo zacht
Kozend, voortliep en dacht:
Hier onder deez' eik is 't goed vrijen,
Kwam een laars van den man,
Die daar boven hing, van
Zijn reeds verteerd linkerbeen glijen.

'Al mijn leven! van waar
Komt die laars?' riep het paar,
En werktuigelijk keek het naar boven.
En daar zag het met schrik
Dien mijnheer, eens zo dik
En nu tot een geraamte afgekloven.

Op zijn grijnzenden kop
Stond zijn hoed nog rechtop,
Maar de rand was eraf. Al zijn linnen
Was gerafeld en grauw.
Door een gat in zijn mouw
Blikten mieren en wurmen en spinnen.

Zijn horloge stond stil
En één glas van zijn bril
Was kapot en het ander beslagen.
Op den rand van een zak
Van zijn vest zat een slak,
Een erg slijmrige slak, stil te knagen.

And the cold winter cleared,
As the springtime appeared,
And in turn to the summer gave way,
A pair strayed – it was very hot –
Arm in arm to the spot
In the wood, but see their dismay!

While they had their sweet sport,
And caressed, walked and thought:
Here under this oak's good for hiding,
An large boot from the guy,
Who was hanging on high,
Off his rotten left leg now came gliding.

'My life's love, oh from where
Came that boot?' cried the pair,
And instinctively looked to the sky.
Their sheer horror was great:
The gent, once overweight,
Was reduced to a skeleton, dry.

On his grimacing pate
His hat still stood straight,
But the brim had come off and his shirt
Was threadbare, grey as ash.
In his sleeve was a gash,
Whence peeped ants, worms and spiders, alert.

Both his watch hands had stopped,
And one lens glass had popped,
While the other had misted completely,
On one fob pocket's edge,
On its own little ledge,
Was a slimy snail, gnawing discreetly.

In een wip was de lust
Om te vrijen geblust
Bij het paar. Zelfs geen word dorst het spreken.
't Zag van schrik zóó spierwit
Als een laken, wen dit
Reeds een dag op het gras ligt te bleeken.

In a trice the desire
To make love lost its fire
In the pair. They were robbed of all speech.
Both were pallid with fright
As a sheet of pure white
Left a day on the meadow to bleach.

Troost

Laat vallen 't purperrood gordijn!
Ik wil met droomen zalig zijn.

O, neem mijn hand en streel mijn haar,
Dan wordt mijn hart weer achttien jaar.

En fluister woorden zonder zin:
Daar vond ik eens mijn hemel in.

En leg beloften in uw lach
En leer mij lieven als ik plach.

En blik me in de oogen zoals hij
En doe dat ál uit medelij.

O, lieve, lieve, wees niet boos,
Omdat ik denk aan hem altoos!

Maar lieg als hij en streel mijn haar,
Dan wordt mijn hart weer achttien jaar.

HÉLÈNE SWARTH 1859–1941

CONSOLATION

Let the deep-crimson curtain fall!
Let dreams my present life enthrall.

Oh, take my hand and stroke my hair,
A heart of eighteen I'll then wear.

And whisper words that make no sense:
Once heaven was not more intense.

And put a promise in your smile,
Teach me to love you as erstwhile,

And like him look me in the eyes
And out of pity tell me lies,

O darling, darling, don't be grim
Because I always think of him!

But lie like him and stroke my hair,
A heart of eighteen I'll then wear.

DE BOMEN DORREN IN HET LAAT SEIZOEN

De bomen dorren in het laat seizoen,
En wachten roerloos den nabijen winter...
Wat is dat alles stil, doodstil... ik vind er
Mijn *eigen* leven in, dat heen gaat spoên.

Ach, 'k had zo graag heel, héél veel willen doen,
Wat Verzen en wat Liefde, – want wie mint er
Te sterven zonder dees? Maar wie ook wint er
Ter wereld iets door klagen of door woên?

Ik ga dan stil, tevreden en gedwee,
En neem geen ding uit al dat Leven meê
Dan dees gedachte, gonzende in mij om:

Men moet niet van het lieve Dood-zijn ijzen:
De dode bloemen komen niet weêrom,
Maar Ik zal heerlijk in mijn Vers herrijzen.

The Trees Are Wilting At The Season's End

The trees are wilting at the season's end,
Awaiting motionless the approaching winter...
How still it all is, deathly still... The stint of
My *own* brief life's contained there, almost spent.

Ah, much, so much I dearly would have done,
Some Verses and some Love, – for who is eager
Without them to face death? But who by meagre
Rage or complaint has something ever won?

Contented, still and meek I now will be,
And nothing from that Life I take with me
Than this thought that is pounding in my brain:

One need not shudder at one's own fond Death:
The dead flowers will not ever come again,
But I will in my Verse once more draw breath.

Kent Iemand Dat Gevoel

Kent iemand dat gevoel: 't is geen verdriet,
't is geen geluk, geen menging van die beiden;
't hangt over je, om je, als wolken over heiden,
stil, hoog, licht, ernstig; ze bewegen niet.

Je voelt je kind en oud; je denken ziet
door alles, wat scheen je van God te scheiden.
't Is, of een punt tot cirkel gaat verwijden;
't is, of een cirkel punt wordt en verschiet.

Je denkt: Nooit was het anders; tot mijn Wezen
ben 'k al zo lang van sterflijkheid genezen.
Je weet: Niets kan mij deren; ik ben Hij.

Tot zekerheid je twijfel opgeheven,
zo hang je als eeuwig boven je eigen leven:
je bent de wolken en je bent de hei.

Who Knows That Feeling

Who knows that feeling: it is not distress,
not joy, nor yet a mixture of the two;
like heathland clouds it hangs round, over you:
still, high, light, serious; and motionless.

You feel a child yet old; you grasp aright
what you from God once seemed to separate.
As if a dot to circle will dilate,
circle contract to dot, shoot off from sight.

You think: Nothing has changed; to my true Being
I've long been cured from my mortality.
You know: Nothing can harm me; I am He.

You rise above your doubt to certain seeing,
hang as eternal, your whole life beneath:
you are the high clouds and you are the heath.

DE STILLE WEG

De stille weg
de maannachtlichte weg –

de boomen
de zoo stil oudgeworden boomen –
het water
het zachtbespannen tevree' water.

En daar achter in 't ver de neergezonken hemel
met 't sterrengefemel.

THE SILENT ROAD

The silent road
the glowing moonlit road –

the trees
the oh so still and aged trees –
the water
the gently tautened contented water,

And beyond, far off, the sunken sky
with the stars' wheedling cry.

Om Mijn Oud Woonhuis Peppels Staan

Om mijn oud woonhuis peppels staan
'mijn lief, mijn lief, o waar gebleven'
een smalle laan
van natte blaren, het vallen komt.

Het regent, regent eender te hooren
'mijn lief, mijn lief, o waar gebleven'
en altijd door en
den treuren uit, de wind verstomt.

Het huis is hol en vol duisternis
'mijn lief, mijn lief, o waar gebleven'
gefluister is
boven op zolder, het dakgebint.

Er woont er een voorovergebogen
'mijn lief, mijn lief, o waar gebleven'
met leege oogen
en die zijn vrede en rust niet vindt.

ROUND MY OLD HOUSE TALL POPLARS CRANE

Round my old house tall poplars crane
'my love, my love, where are you now'
a narrow lane
of wet leaves, and the fall to come.

And on and on the dull refrain
'my love, my love, where are you now'
of rain on rain
past grieving, and the wind is dumb.

The house is hollow, dark and bleak
'my love, my love, where are you now'
with whispered creaks
of attic beams that will not cease.

Inside sits someone hunched and lined
'my love, my love, where are you now'
whose eyes are blind
whose mind finds neither rest nor peace.

DE TERRASSEN VAN MEUDON

De lucht is stil: op eindloos verre heuvlen
Strekt zich de stad in blond en rozig licht –
Ik wend mij om waar lachen klinkt en keuvlen:
Daar kust een knaap een blank en zoet gezicht.

Ik zie omlaag: in vaste en strenge perken
Sombert rondom een kom een herfstge tuin.
Ik zie omhoog: een koepel, zwaar van zerken,
Stijgt, sterrewacht, hoog boven de bomenkruin.

Op trapgesteenten, broklig, maar gebleven,
Blijf ik dan peinzend en weemoedig staan –
Want dode dingen zijn die langer leven
Dan wij die werden, welken en vergaan.

ALBERT VERWEY 1865–1937

The Terraces Of Meudon

The air is still: on endlessly far slopes
The city extends in blond and rosy light –
I'm drawn to sounds of mirth and chatty tropes:
A young man kisses a face sweet and white.

Looking down, beds fixed and severe I see:
A stark autumn garden round a basin lies.
Looking up: a dome, full of tombs and history,
Like an observatory above the treetops flies.

A stone flight of steps that crumbles yet survives
Makes me pause in melancholy thought –
For lifeless things may still have longer lives
Than we who've grown and fade and come to nought.

NACHT-STILTE

Stil, wees stil: op zilvren voeten
Schrijdt de stilte door den nacht,
Stilte die der goden groeten
Overbrengt naar lage wacht...
Wat niet ziel tot ziel kon spreken
Door der dagen ijl gegons,
Spreekt uit overluchtsche streken,
Klaar als ster in licht zoû breken,
Zonder smet van taal of teeken
God in elk van ons.

Night-Silence

Hush now, hush: on feet of silver
Through the night see silence go,
Silence that from gods delivers
Greetings to the watch below...
What 'twixt souls could not be spoken
In the daytime's empty din,
From high realms that night has woken,
Into light star-bright now broken,
Sullied by no word or token
God speaks deep within.

Het Huwelijk

Toen hij bespeurde hoe de nevel van den tijd
in d'oogen van zijn vrouw de vonken uit kwam dooven,
haar wangen had verweerd, haar voorhoofd had doorkloven
toen wendde hij zich af en vrat zich op van spijt.

Hij vloekte en ging te keer en trok zich bij den baard
en mat haar met den blik, maar kon niet meer begeeren,
hij zag de grootsche zonde in duivelsplicht verkeeren
en hoe zij tot hem opkeek als een stervend paard.

Maar sterven deed zij niet al zoog zijn helsche mond
het merg uit maar gebeente, dat haar tòch bleef dragen
Zij dorst niet spreken meer, niet vragen of niet klagen,
en rilde waar zij stond, maar leefde en bleef gezond.

Hij dacht: ik sla haar dood en steek het huis in brand.
Ik moet de schimmel van mijn stramme voeten wasschen
en rennen door het vuur en door het water plassen
tot bij een ander lief in eenig ander land.

Maar doodslaan deed hij niet, want tusschen droom en daad
staan wetten in de weg en praktische bezwaren,
en ook weemoedigheid, die niemand kan verklaren,
en die des avonds komt, wanneer men slapen gaat.

Zoo gingen jaren heen. De kindren werden groot
en zagen dat de man die zij hun vader heetten,
bewegingloos en zwijgend bij her vuur gezten,
een godvergeten en vervaarlijk' aanblik bood.

WILLEM ELSSCHOT 1882–1960

The Marriage

Perceiving how the creeping mists of age
had left the sparkle in his wife's eyes quenched,
her cheeks all worn, her forehead deeply trenched,
he turned away and fumed in helpless rage.

Furiously tugging at his beard he'd swear
survey her, with no passion left to feel,
see sin once splendid turn to an ordeal,
while she gazed up like some poor dying mare.

She would not die; though like a fiend from hell
he sucked her marrowbones, they'd still not crack.
Afraid to whine, beseech or answer back,
she shook with fear, yet stayed alive and well.

He thought: I'll kill her, set the house ablaze.
I'll wash the mildew off my stiffening frame,
escape through water and through cleansing flame,
and find new love, new pastures I can graze.

And yet he didn't kill, as giving dreams their head
raises both practical and legal snags,
and, puzzlingly, one's spirit always flags
when evening comes and it is time for bed.

His children grew, as year on year passed by,
and saw how the man whom they called their sire
sat motionless and tight-lipped by the fire
with godforsaken grimness in his eye.

DE DAPPERSTRAAT

Natuur is voor tevredenen of legen.
En dan: wat is natuur nog in dit land?
Een stukje bos, ter grootte van een krant,
Een heuvel met wat villaatjes ertegen.

Geef mij de grauwe, stedelijke wegen,
De in kaden vastgeklonken waterkant,
De wolken, nooit zo schoon dan als ze, omrand
Door zolderramen, langs de lucht bewegen.

Alles is veel voor wie niet veel verwacht.
Het leven houdt zijn wonderen verborgen
Tot het ze, opeens, toont in hun hoge staat.

Dit heb ik bij mijzelven overdacht,
Verregend, op een miezerige morgen,
Domweg gelukkig, in de Dapperstraat.

THE DAPPERSTRAAT

Nature is for the blank or satisfied.
And then: what can we boast of naturewise?
A stretch of woodland, postage stamp in size,
A hill with some small houses on the side.

Give me the town roads with their greyish cast,
The harbour quays of interlocking stone
The clouds whose beauty cannot be outdone
When, skylight-framed, they all go drifting past.

Everything's much if much is not expected.
Life hides its miracles till, without warning,
They're suddenly displayed in all their art.

This on my own I thought I had detected,
Rain-sodden, on a drab and drizzly morning,
Just downright happy, in the Dapperstraat.

DE TUINMAN EN DE DOOD

Een Perzisch Edelman:

Van morgen ijlt mijn tuinman, wit van schrik,
Mijn woning in: 'Heer, Heer, één ogenblik!

Ginds, in de rooshof, snoeide ik loot na loot,
Toen keek ik achter mij. Daar stond de Dood.

Ik schrok, en haastte mij langs de andre kant,
Maar zag nog juist de dreiging van zijn hand.

Meester, uw paard, en laat mij spoorslags gaan,
Voor de avond nog bereik ik Ispahaan!' –

Van middag – lang reeds was hij heengespoed –
Heb ik in 't cederpark de Dood ontmoet.

'Waarom', zo vraag ik, want hij wacht en zwijgt,
'Hebt gij van morgen vroeg mijn knecht gedreigd?'

Glimlachend antwoordt hij: 'Geen dreiging was 't,
Waarvoor uw tuinman vlood. Ik was verrast,

Toen 'k 's morgens hier nog stil aan 't werk zag staan,
Die 'k 's avonds halen moest in Ispahaan.'

P.N. VAN EYCK 1887–1954

THE GARDENER AND DEATH

A Persian nobleman:

This morning, white with fear, my gardener flees
Into my house: 'Master, a moment please!

Out in the rose-beds, pruning shoots with care,
I looked behind me. Death was standing there.

I gave a start, and sought my getaway,
But glimpsed his hand that made as if to slay.

Master, your horse, and at full tilt I'll ride,
Ere evening comes, in Isfahan I'll hide!' –

This afternoon – long since he off had set –
Amongst the cedars Death I also met.

'Why', I inquire, since he waits silently,
'Did you my servant treat so threateningly?'

Smiling he said: 'A threat caused in no wise
Your gardener to flee. I showed surprise

To find still here and busy just the man
This evening I must fetch in Isfahan.'

De Moeder De Vrouw

Ik ging naar Bommel om de brug te zien.
Ik zag de nieuwe brug. Twee overzijden
die elkaar vroeger schenen te vermijden
worden weer buren. Een minuut of tien
dat ik daar lag, in 't gras, mijn thee gedronken
mijn hoofd vol van het landschap wijd en zijd –
laat mij daar midden uit de oneindigheid
een stem vernemen dat mijn oren klonken.

Het was een vrouw. Het schip dat zij bevoer
kwam langzaamaan stroomaf door de brug gevaren.
Zij was alleen aan dek, zij stond bij 't roer,

en wat zij zong hoorde ik dat psalmen waren.
O, dacht ik, o dat daar mijn moeder voer.
Prijs God zong zij, Zijn hand zal u bewaren.

MARTINUS NIJHOFF 1894–1953

'THE OLD LADY'

I went to Bommel just to see the bridge.
I saw the new bridge. Two opposing shores
that shunned each other seemingly before
are neighbours once again. A grassy verge
I lay on, tea consumed, for some ten minutes
my head filled with the landscape far and wide –
when from that endlessness on every side
this voice came, and my ears resounded with it.

It was a woman. And the boat she steered
was passing downstream through the bridge quite slowly.
She stood there at the helm, alone on deck,

and what she sang were hymns, I now could hear.
Oh, I thought, oh, were mother there instead.
Praise God she sang, His hand shall safely hold thee.

MELOPEE

Voor Gaston Burssens

Onder de maan schuift de lange rivier
Over de lange rivier schuift moede de maan
Onder de maan op de lange rivier schuift de kano naar zee

Langs het hoogriet
langs de laagwei
schuift de kano naar zee
schuift met de schuivende maan de kano naar zee
Zo zijn ze gezellen naar zee de kano de maan en de man
Waarom schuiven de maan en de man getweeën gedwee
    naar de zee

PAUL VAN OSTAIJEN 1896–1928

MELOPEE

for Gaston Burssens

Under the moon the long river slides
Over the long river the spent moon slides
Under the moon on the long river the canoe slides to the sea

Past the high sedge
past the low fields
the canoe slides to the sea
the canoe slides with the sliding moon to the sea
So they're companions to the sea the canoe the moon and
 the man
Why do the moon and the man slide paired and subdued
 to the sea

WONINGLOZE

Alleen in mijn gedichten kan ik wonen,
Nooit vond ik ergens anders onderdak;
Voor de eigen haard gevoelde ik nooit een zwak,
Een tent werd door de stormwind meegenomen.

Alleen in mijn gedichten kan ik wonen.
Zolang ik weet dat ik in wildernis,
In steppen, stad en woud dat onderkomen
Kan vinden, deert mij geen bekommernis.

Het zal lang duren, maar de tijd zal komen
Dat vóór de nacht mij de oude kracht ontbreekt
En tevergeefs om zachte woorden smeekt,
Waarmee 'k weleer kon bouwen, en de aarde
Mij bergen moet en ik mij neerbuig naar de
Plek waar mijn graf in 't donker openbreekt.

J. SLAUERHOFF 1898–1936

HOMELESS

My poems are my only habitation,
No other shelter could I ever find;
Homesick yearnings never fill my mind,
Tents cannot withstand the tempest's devastation.

My poems are my only habitation.
While I still know that in the wilderness,
In steppes, towns, woods or somewhere in creation
A roof is to be found, there's no distress.

Some distant day will bring the consummation:
Before night comes my former strength will fade,
Vainly I'll summon soft words to my aid,
Once my building blocks; my accommodation
Will be in the earth, and in deep prostration
I'll bow to where my grave gapes in the shade.

Herinnering Aan Holland

Denkend aan Holland
zie ik brede rivieren
traag door oneindig
laagland gaan,
rijen ondenkbaar
ijle populieren
als hoge pluimen
aan de einder staan;
en in de geweldige
ruimte verzonken
de boerderijen
verspreid door het land,
boomgroepen, dorpen,
geknotte torens,
kerken en olmen
in een groots verband.
de lucht hangt er laag
en de zon wordt er langzaam
in grijze veelkleurige
dampen gesmoord,
en in alle gewesten
wordt de stem van het water
met zijn eeuwige rampen
gevreesd en gehoord.

H. MARSMAN 1899–1940

MEMORY OF HOLLAND

Thinking of Holland
I see wide-flowing rivers
slowly traversing
infinite plains,
inconceivably
rarefied poplars
like lofty plumes
on the skyline in lanes;
and submerged in the vastness
of unbounded spaces
the farmhouses
strewn through the land,
tree clumps, villages,
truncated towers,
churches and elm trees
all wondrously planned.
the sky hangs low
and slowly the sun by
mists of all colours
is stifled and greyed
and in all the regions
the voice of the water
with its endless disasters
is feared and obeyed.

VERA JANACOPOULOS

Cantilene

Ambrosia, wat vloeit mij aan?
uw schedelveld is koeler maan
en alle appels blozen

de klankgazelle die ik vond
hoe zoete zoele kindermond
van zeeschuim en van rozen

o muze in het morgenlicht
o minnares en slank gedicht
er is een god verscholen

violen vlagen op het mos
elysium, de vlinders los
en duizendjarig dolen

JAN ENGELMAN 1900–1972

VERA JANACOPOULOS

Vocolise

Ambrosia, my honey spoon?
your skull is cooler than the moon
and every apple's blushing

the sound gazelle I chanced to meet
such a child's mouth, sultry and sweet,
of sea foam and roses rushing

o my muse in the morning light
o lover and a poem, slight
a godhead disappears

upon the moss a violin sighs
elysium, free the butterflies
and roam for a thousand years.

JACHTOPZIENER

Ik kwam vandaag de jachtopziener tegen
en vroeg hem naar de stand van het roodwild.
Hij draaide er om heen en trok verlegen
met een schoenpunt raadsels in het grint.

Ik was hem sinds zijn aanstelling genegen
en hij mij wederkerig goedgezind.
Waarom werd ik opeens geheel ontsteld,
of hij reeds maanden iets had doodgezwegen?

Er is er altijd één meer dan ik tel,
zei hij bezorgd en keek me in de ogen.
Waanzin en waarheid lagen in de zijne
voortdurend voor elkander te verschijnen.
De bomen stonden naar ons toegebogen.
Toen klonk ginds op het huis de etensbel.

GERRIT ACHTERBERG 1905–1962

GAMEKEEPER

I chanced to meet my gamekeeper of late
and asked about the shape the deer were in.
He hummed and hawed and drew a bashful spate
of runic signs in gravel with his shoe.

I'd liked the man since his appointment date;
the goodwill seemed to be quite mutual too.
Why was I thrown completely in a spin,
as if he'd long failed to communicate?

There's often one more than the count should be,
he said concerned and looked me in the eye.
In his, insanity and truth ran free
and jockeyed for position constantly.
The trees inclined towards us from the sky,
Then from afar the house bell rang for tea.

Het Carillon

Ik zag de mensen in de straten,
hun armoe en hun grauw gezicht, –
toen streek er over de gelaten
een luisteren, een vleug van licht.

Want boven in de klokketoren
na 't donker-bronzen urenslaan
ving, over heel de stad te horen,
de beiaardier te spelen aan.

Valerius : – een statig zingen
waarin de zware klok bewoog,
doorstrooid van lichter sprankelingen,
'Wij slaan het oog tot U omhoog.'

En één tussen de naamloos velen,
gedrongen aan de huizenkant
stond ik te luist'ren naar dit spelen
dat zong van mijn geschonden land.

Dit sprakeloze samenkomen
en Hollands licht over de stad –
Nooit heb ik wat ons werd ontnomen
zo bitter, bitter liefgehad.

Oorlogsjaar 1941

IDA GERHARDT 1905–1997

The Carillon

The people in the streets looked stricken,
their ashen faces drawn and tight, –
then something made their features quicken
and, listening, they seemed brushed with light.

For in the clock-tower when, resounding,
the bronze-chimed hour had died away,
the carilloneur began his pounding
and everywhere was heard to play.

Valerius: – a solemn singing
with bass bell's tolling undertone
and flickerings of lighter ringing:
'We raise our eyes to Thy high throne.'

As one of all those nameless people
who by the house fronts came to stand,
I listened to the pealing steeple
that sang of my afflicted land.

This speechless gathering, beyond us
the city with Dutch light above –
I've never for what's stolen from us
felt such a bitter, bitter love.

War year 1941

De Idioot In Het Bad

Met opgetrokken schouders, toegeknepen ogen,
haast dravend en vaak hakend in de mat,
lelijk en onbeholpen aan zusters arm gebogen,
gaat elke week de idioot naar 't bad.

De damp, die van het warme water slaat
maakt hem geruster: witte stoom...
En bij elk kledingstuk, dat van hem afgaat,
bevangt hem meer en meer een oud vertrouwde droom.

De zuster laat hem in het water glijden,
hij vouwt zijn dunne armen op zijn borst,
hij zucht, als bij het lessen van zijn eerste dorst
en om zijn mond gloort langzaamaan een groot verblijden.

Zijn zorgelijk gezicht is leeg en mooi geworden,
zijn dunne voeten staan rechtop als bleke bloemen,
zijn lange, bleke benen, die reeds licht verdorden
komen als berkenstammen door het groen opdoemen.

Hij is in dit groen water nog als ongeboren,
hij weet nog niet, dat sommige vruchten nimmer rijpen,
hij heeft de wijsheid van het lichaam niet verloren
en hoeft de dingen van de geest niet te begrijpen.

En elke keer, dat hij uit 't bad gehaald wordt,
en stevig met een handdoek drooggewreven
en in zijn stijve, harde kleren wordt gesjord
stribbelt hij tegen en dan huilt hij even.

THE IDIOT IN THE BATH

With both his shoulders hunched and eyelids screwed up tight,
jogging, tripping on the mats in his path,
bending on sister's arm now, an ugly, clumsy sight,
the idiot goes to take his weekly bath.

The vapour rising from the water's heat
calms him somewhat: pure white steam...
And as each new garment falls down at his feet,
the more he's caught up in a long-familiar dream.

Into the tub the sister helps him slide,
his spindly arms across his chest are clenched,
he sighs as if his first keen thirst has now been quenched
and as it slowly glows his happy mouth grins wide.

Vacant and serene is the face that feared and dithered,
thin feet stick up like flowers, with a pallid sheen,
his long and pale legs, already slightly withered,
both come looming up like birch trunks amid the green.

He is in this green water still like an embryo,
still unaware there are some fruits that ripeness never find,
he has not yet lost the wisdom that our bodies know
and has no need to grasp the workings of the mind.

Whenever he's evicted from his bath-time sloth,
and he is briskly rubbed dry with a towel,
and he is jerked into the stiff, unyielding cloth,
he resists feebly and has a little howl.

149

En elke week wordt hij opnieuw geboren
en wreed gescheiden van het veilig water-leven
en elke week is hem het lot beschoren opnieuw een bange
idioot te zijn gebleven.

And every week he's once again reborn,
and is cruelly divorced from his safe water-glade,
and every week this fate has to be borne, of being just an
idiot again, afraid.

Niet Ongelijk

Niet ongelijk is de lijn van je ogen
aan de lijnen van meeuwen of vooral die van visdiefjes
Toeval? Een romantisch bewijs voor één Schepper?
Ik weet niet Wel weet ik dat je ogen al lang weer
ver weg zijn gevlogen Zonder spoor of contact
zomin als kiekendieven of de langzaam maar zekere
    tochten
van spitsgevleugelde valken iets te maken hebben
met de treinen die ze passeren.

NOT UNLIKE

The line of your eyes is not unlike
the lines of seagulls or especially of terns
Coincidence? Romantic evidence of one Creator?
I don't know What I do know is that your eyes have long
    since
flown far away Without trace or contact
as little as harriers or the slow but sure passages
of pointed-winged falcons are connected
with the trains that they pass.

BLOEMEN

Als alle mensen eensklaps bloemen waren
zouden zij grote bloemen zijn met lange snorren.
Vermagerde vliegen, dode torren
zouden blijven haken in hun haren.
Tandenstokers, steelsgewijs ontsproten,
zouden zwellen tot gedraaide tafelpoten,
katoenen knoppen zouden openscheuren
tot pluche harten die naar franje geuren,

en op de bergen zouden gipsen zuilen staan
die gipsen druiven huilen.

Op het water dreven bordkartonnen blaren,
de vlinders vielen uit elkaar tot losse vlerken
en van geur verdorden alle perken
als alle mensen eensklaps bloemen waren.

Flowers

If everyone turned all at once to flowers
they would be large-sized flowers with trailing whiskers.
Emaciated flies, dead beetles
would end entangled in their hairs.
Toothpicks, surreptitiously sprouted
would swell into turned table-legs,
buds of cotton would burst open
into plush hearts that smelled of fringes,

and on the mountains plaster pillars stand
weeping spates of plaster grapes.

Cardboard leaves would drift upon the water,
the butterflies fall apart into loose wings
and all the flowerbeds shrivel up with scent
if everyone turned all at once to flowers.

Ik Denk

ik denk
als het regent
laat ze niet nat worden

en als het stormt
vat ze geen kou

en ik denk ook
dat dat denken
niet helpt

want je wordt nooit meer
nat noch vat je een kou

want het regent
noch waait ooit
meer voor jou

BERT SCHIERBEEK 1918–1996

I Think

I think
when it rains
don't let her get wet

and when there's a storm
she won't catch cold

and I also think
that that thinking's
no help

since you'll never get wet
again or catch a cold

because it will never
rain or blow
on you again

BOMMEN

De stad is stil.
De straten
hebben zich verbreed.
Kangeroes kijken door de venstergaten.
Een vrouw passeert.
De echo raapt gehaast
haar stappen op.

De stad is stil.
Een kat rolt stijf van het kozijn.
Het licht is als een blok verplaatst.
Geruisloos vallen drie vier bommen op het plein
en drie vier huizen hijsen traag
hun rode vlag.

PAUL RODENKO 1920–1976

BOMBS

The city's quiet.
The streets
have widened.
Kangaroos peer through the window openings.
A woman passes.
The echo hastily picks up
her steps.

The city's still.
A cat rolls stiffly off the windowsill.
The light has shifted like a block.
Noiselessly three or four bombs fall on the square
and three or four houses slowly hoist
their red flags.

Onzichtbaar

Onzichtbaar
kom je mij tegemoet
op mijn moeizame tocht
door het maanlandschap
van de tijd.

Onhoorbaar
dringt je stem door
tot mijn geheimste
luisterpost.

Jij die al mijn wegen kent,
die mij ontcijferd en gelezen hebt,
blijf bij mij
onzichtbaar, onhoorbaar
en leid mij over de drempel
van de dood.

HANNY MICHAELIS 1922–2007

INVISIBLY

Invisibly
you come to meet me
on my arduous journey
through the lunar landscape
of time.

Inaudibly
your voice penetrates
my most secret
listening post.

You who know all my ways,
who have deciphered and read me,
stay with me
invisibly, inaudibly
and lead me across the threshold
of death.

Totaal Witte Kamer

Laten wij nog eenmaal de kamer wit maken
nog eenmaal de totaal witte kamer, jij, ik

dit zal geen tijd sparen, maar nog eenmaal
de kamer wit maken, nu, nooit meer later

en dat we dan bijna het volmaakte napraten
alsof het gedrukt staat, witter dan leesbaar

dus nog eenmaal die kamer, de voor altijd totale
zoals wij er lagen, liggen, liggen blijven
witter dan, samen –

GERRIT KOUWENAAR 1923–2014

TOTALLY WHITE ROOM

Let's make the room white one last time
one last time the totally white room, you, I

this won't save any time, but let's make the room
white one last time, now, never again later

and then almost echoing perfection
as if it is printed, whiter than legible

so one last time that room, the eternally total
as we lay there, lie, remain lying
whiter than, together –

Ik Tracht Op Poëtische Wijze

ik tracht op poëtische wijze
dat wil zeggen
eenvouds verlichte waters
de ruimte van het volledig leven
tot uitdrukking te brengen

ware ik geen mens geweest
gelijk aan menigte mensen
maar ware ik die ik was
de stenen of vloeibare engel
geboorte en ontbinding hadden mij niet aangeraakt
de weg van verlatenheid naar gemeenschap
de stenen stenen dieren dieren vogels vogels weg
zo niet zo bevuild zijn
als dat nu te zien is aan mijn gedichten
die momentopnamen zijn van die weg

in deze tijd heeft wat men altijd noemde
schoonheid schoonheid haar gezicht verbrand
zij troost niet meer de mensen
zij troost de larven de reptielen de ratten
maar de mens verschrikt zij
en treft hem met het besef
een broodkruimel te zijn op de rok van het universum

niet meer alleen het kwade
de doodsteek maakt ons opstandig of deemoedig
maar ook het goede
de omarming laat ons wanhopig aan de ruimte
morrelen

I Try In Poetic Ways

I try in poetic ways
that is
simplicity's luminous waters
to express
the breadth of life's totality

had I not been a man
like hosts of other men
but if I were who I was
the stone or liquid angel
birth and decay would not have touched me
the road from abandonment to community
the stones stones creatures creatures birds birds road
would not have been as soiled
as can now be seen from my poems
which are still photos of that road

in this age what was always called
beauty beauty has burnt its face
it no longer consoles people
it consoles the larvae the reptiles the rats
but people it terrifies
and strikes them with the sense
of being a crumb on the universe's skirt

it's no longer just evil
the fatal thrust that makes us rebellious or humble
but good too
embraces make us tamper desperately
with space

ik heb daarom de taal
in haar schoonheid opgezocht
hoorde daar dat zij niet meer menselijks had
dan de spraakgebreken van de schaduw
dan die van het oorverdovend zonlicht

so that's why I
sought out language in its beauty
heard that there was nothing human left in it
but the speech impediments of shadow
but those of ear-shattering sunlight

DE LEGE KAMER BLIJFT DE LEGE KAMER

De lege kamer blijft de lege kamer.
Alleen ikzelf er in en niemand opent
de deur, geen vrouw of vriend, geen vreemde.
Ik heb dit eerder meegemaakt maar nu
ben ik al zoveel jaren ouder
en valt het zoveel moeilijker te geloven
dat dit weer overgaat, dat ik zal lopen
misschien niet vrij van deze zieke man maar toch
weer in het licht waarvan ik heb gehouden.

HANS ANDREUS 1926–1977

THE EMPTY ROOM REMAINS THE EMPTY ROOM

The empty room remains the empty room.
Only me in it and no one opens
the door, no woman or friend, no stranger.
I've been through this before but now
I am so many years older
and it's so much more difficult to believe
that this will pass, that I shall walk
perhaps not free of this sick man but still
in the light again which I have loved.

Poëzie Is Een Daad

Poëzie is een daad
van bevestiging. Ik bevestig
dat ik leef, dat ik niet alleen leef.

Poëzie is een toekomst, denken
aan de volgende week, aan een ander land,
aan jou als je oud bent.

Poëzie is mijn adem, beweegt
mijn voeten, aarzelend soms,
over de aarde die daarom vraagt.

Voltaire had pokken, maar
genas zichzelf door o.a te drinken
120 liter limonade: dat is poëzie.

Of neem de branding. Stukgeslagen
op de rotsen is zij niet werkelijk verslagen,
maar herneemt zich en is daarin poëzie.

Elk woord dat wordt geschreven
is een aanslag op de ouderdom.
Ten slotte wint de dood, jazeker,

maar de dood is slechts de stilte in de zaal
nadat het laatste woord geklonken heeft.
De dood is een ontroering.

POETRY IS AN ACT

Poetry is an act
of affirmation. I affirm
I'm alive, that I'm not alone.

Poetry is a future, thinking
of next week, of another country,
of you when you're old.

Poetry is my breath, moves
my feet, hesitantly at times,
across the earth that needs it.

Voltaire had smallpox, but
cured himself, for example, by drinking
120 litres of lemonade: that's poetry.

Or take the surf. Smashed to pieces
on the rocks it is isn't really defeated,
but regroups and so becomes poetry.

Every word that's written
is an assault on old age.
Death wins in the end, of course,

but death is only the silence in the hall,
after the last word has sounded.
Death is an emotion.

In Flanders Fields

De grond is hier het vetst.
Zelfs na al die jaren zonder mest
zou je hier een dodenprei kunnen kweken
die alle markten tart.

De wankele Engelse veteranen worden schaars.
Elk jaar wijzen zij aan hun schaarsere vrienden:
Hill Sixty, Hill Sixty One, Poelkapelle.

In Flanders Fields rijden de maaldorsers
steeds dichtere kringen rond de kronkelgangen
van verharde zandzakken, de darmen van de dood.

De boter van de streek
smaakt naar klaprozen.

In Flanders Fields

Here the soil is most rank.
Even after all these years without dung
you could raise a prize death leek here
to challenge any market.

The English veterans are getting scarce.
Every year they point to their yet scarcer friends:
Hill Sixty, Hill Sixty-One, Poelkapelle.

In Flanders Fields the threshers
draw ever smaller circles round the twisting trenches
of hardened sandbags, the entrails of death.

The local butter
tastes of poppies.

ZODRA IK MIJN OGEN OPSLA

Zodra ik mijn ogen opsla
is het onzichtbare mij ontglipt
en begin ik te zien wat ik zie:
herinneringen aan wat ik zag

en ooit al zal zien. Door te zien
blijf ik mij herinneren;

en hoop ik dat ik besta.

Vooral als ik naar haar kijk
wanneer zij zo haar hand door
haar haar haalt, haar elleboog
steunend op haar knie, en zij
iets tegen mij zegt.

THE MOMENT I RAISE MY EYES

The moment I raise my eyes
the invisible's eluded me
and I begin to see what I see:
memories of what I saw

and will one day see. By seeing
I go on remembering;

I hope I exist.

Especially when I look at her
as she runs her hand through
her hair that way, her elbow
resting on her knee, and she
says something to me.

Een Kinderspiegel

'Als ik oud word neem ik blonde krullen
ik neem geen spataders, geen onderkin,
en als ik rimpels krijg omdat ik vijftig ben
dan neem ik vrolijke, niet van die lange om mijn mond
alleen wat kraaiepootjes om mijn ogen.

Ik ga nooit liegen of bedriegen, waarom zou ik
en niemand gaat ooit liegen tegen mij.
Ik neem niet van die vieze vette
grijze pieken en ik ga zeker ook niet
stinken uit mijn mond.

Ik neem een hond, drie poezen en een geit
die binnen mag, dat is gezellig,
de keutels kunnen mij niet schelen.
De poezen mogen in mijn bed
de hond gaat op het kleedje.

Ik neem ook hele leuke planten met veel bloemen
niet van die saaie sprieten en geen luis, of zoiets raars.
Ik neem een hele lieve man die tamelijk beroemd is
de hele dag en ook de hele nacht
blijven wij alsmaar bij elkaar.'

A Child's Mirror

'When I'm old I'll have blond curls
I won't have varicose veins, or a double chin,
and if I have wrinkles because I'm fifty
I'll have cheerful ones, not those long ones round my
    mouth
just some crow's feet round my eyes.

I'll never lie or deceive, why should I
and no one will ever lie to me.
I won't have those dirty greasy
grey wisps of hair and I certainly won't
have bad breath.

I'll have a dog, three cats and a goat
that's allowed inside, that's cosy,
the droppings won't bother me.
The cats can sleep in my bed
the dog goes on the mat.

I'll have really nice plants too with lots of flowers
not those dreary shoots and no lice, or anything weird
    like that.
I'll have a very sweet husband who is quite well known
all day and all night long
we'll be together the whole time.'

Onder De Appelboom

Ik kwam thuis, het was
een uur of acht en zeldzaam
zacht voor de tijd van het jaar,
de tuinbank stond klaar
onder de appelboom

ik ging zitten en ik zat
te kijken hoe de buurman
in zijn tuin nog aan het spitten
was, de nacht kwam uit de aarde
een blauwer wordend licht hing
in de appelboom

toen werd het langzaam weer te mooi
om waar te zijn, de dingen
van de dag verdwenen voor de geur
van hooi, er lag weer speelgoed
in het gras en verweg in het huis
lachten de kinderen in het bad
tot waar ik zat, tot
onder de appelboom

en later hoorde ik vleugels
van ganzen in de hemel
hoorde ik hoe stil en leeg
het aan het worden was

gelukkig kwam er iemand naast mij
zitten, om precies te zijn jij
was het die naast mij kwam
onder de appelboom, zeldzaam
zacht en dichtbij
voor onze leeftijd.

UNDER THE APPLE TREE

I came home, it was
nearly eight and unusually mild
for the time of year,
the garden bench stood ready here
under the apple tree

I took a seat and I sat
watching how my neighbour
was still busy digging in his
garden, the night came out of the ground
a light that grew bluer hung
in the apple tree

then slowly it once more grew too lovely
to be true, the objects
of the day were replaced by the scent
of hay, there were once more toys lying
in the grass and far off in the house
the children were laughing in the bath
out to where I sat, out to
under the apple tree

and later I heard wings
of geese in the sky
heard how still and empty
all was becoming

luckily someone came and sat
next to me, you to be exact
it was who came next to me
under the apple tree, unusually
mild and close by
for our time of life.

BIJVOORBEELD HET LICHAAM

Bijvoorbeeld uit een te schrijven zin
staat het op, loopt
in deze of gene richting, zoekt
in de brievenbus of op het aanrecht,
tussen de struiken in de tuin:
iets, een herinnering, een
verwachting, iemand misschien.

Even plotseling
en al haast in paniek
roept het zichzelf tot de orde,
keert terug op zijn plek
om te schrijven, dit:

– maar schrijft niet, kijkt
uit het raam naar de lucht,
naar zich langzaam
uitvegende condensstrepen,
de zweeflucht van meeuwen. Zo
onbestuurbaar vaak
is het lichaam, en wat het wil,
zijn denken bevraagt het, maar
juist dat is bedenkelijk: soms
neemt het voetstoots iets aan,
soms heeft het nog
al wat voeten in de aarde –

Bijvoorbeeld aangaande de ziel:
huist zij in mij of bewoon ik haar slechts,
laat ik haar los straks of
bevrijdt juist zij me van mij?

FOR INSTANCE THE BODY

For instance from an unwritten phrase
it gets up, walks
in this direction or that, searches
the letterbox or draining board,
among the bushes in the garden:
for something, a memory, an
expectation, someone perhaps.

Just as suddenly
and almost in panic
it calls itself to order,
returning to its place
to set it down, this:

– but does not write, looks
outside at the sky,
at some slowly self-
effacing vapour trails,
the gliding of seagulls. So
unmanageable can
the body be, and what it wants,
its thinking questions it, but
that is just the worry: some
things it accepts without question,
other things, though,
are a much greater challenge –

For instance concerning the soul:
am I its house, or merely its lodger,
will I let it go one day or
will it rather break free of me?

Het staat er, maar wie
is de schrijver. Wat
schreef dit op.

It's written, but who
is the writer. What
wrote this down.

HYMNE AAN DE WALNOTENBOOM

Blijf af van de vruchten van de walnotenboom,
schud niet aan zijn takken en zijn stam,
wie zich de vruchten toeëigent, wie beslag legt,
liefdeloos, die zal het niet goed gaan.
Wie de walnotenboom pijnigt, zal omvallen.
Lang leve de walnotenboom, moge hij leven in vreugde.
Hij is de eenhuizige rijkdragende.
Hem kwaad berokkenen is er niet bij.
Het zegel beschermt hem. Het onverzwakte schild houdt
    stand.
Niemand steelt van de walnotenboom.
Die het wel doen die zullen zeker inslapen.
Negen kruiden beschermen de walnotenboom.
Fladder weg, ruisende spoken.
Fladder weg, dertien plagen en pijnen.
Es Yggdrasil moet wel een walnotenboom zijn.
Helder zijn in voorjaar en zomer de bladeren.
Blijf met je licht.

H.H. TER BALKT 1938–2015

HYMN OF PRAISE TO THE WALNUT TREE

Keep your hands off the fruit of the walnut tree,
do not shake its branches or its trunk,
whoever appropriates its fruit, whoever takes possession,
without love, that person shall fare ill.
Whoever torments the walnut tree shall fall down.
Long live the walnut tree, may it live in joy.
It is monocious, prolific.
To cause it harm is simply not on.
The seal protects it. The unbroken shield withstands.
No one steals from the walnut tree.
Those who do so even so shall surely pass away.
Nine spices protect the walnut tree.
Flutter off, you rustling ghosts.
Flutter off, you thirteen plagues and torments.
Ash Yggdrasil may well be a walnut tree.
Vivid in spring and in summer the leaves.
Stay with your light.

Nemrud Dagh

Wrokkig als bejaarde stieren bergen staan
Tot aan de westelijke eufraat
Droogte kerft en tekent wegen vol inskripties.
Ik lift mee vanaf de basis en mâsjallâh
Wat een meisje. We lopen vast
In commagene waar antiochus de anatoliër
Een breed terras met goden dreef

Geen karrespoor en geen kameel. de landrover
Verdomt het; onverstaanbaar praat zij
Voor zich heen, ik vloek een deun alsof ik
Haar niet zie. zon schijnt zonder duur,
Gezamelijke wartaal houdt bijeen.
In het stuur zit teveel speling

Zij wijst op het terras waar vogels
Zijn versteend; gekanteld beeld
Kijkt in gespleten aarde

Hoofden staan gecraqueleerd, verspreid
Tussen de keien,
Staren zwijgend naar de wagen

Breuklijn: grond komt weerszij onder wielen in beweging

Aarde schuift en trekt een net van kouperose
Ogen om ons heen

Het kijken hakt reeds op ons in.
Wij staan duidelijk alleen

Nemrud Dagh

Resentful as aged bulls mountains rise
As far as the western Euphrates
Drought carves roads full of inscriptions.
I get a lift from the base and mashallah
What a girl. We get stuck
In commagene where antiochus the anatolian
Cut a wide terrace full of gods

Not a cart track nor a camel. The landrover
Can't take it; she talks incomprehensibly
To herself, I hum cursing as if I
Don't see her. sun shines endlessly,
Mutual gibberish is a bond.
There's too much play in the wheel

She points to a terrace where birds
Have petrified; toppled statue
Peers into fissured earth

Heads are craqueléd, scattered
Among the boulders.
Stare silently at the car

Fault line: earth starts moving under wheels on either side

Earth shifts and draws a net of couperose
Eyes around us

The looking is already battering us.
We are clearly alone

Een Locomotief

Er staat een locomotief op een zijspoor,
tot in haar merg verroest, met distels overgroeid.

Als het regent weent zij bruine tranen.

Ik loop langs haar, raak haar aan,
aai haar,
zeg iets tegen haar, iets bemoedigends
klim op de resten van een treeplank.

In de verte slaat een klok.
Misschien ben ik wel een prins. Je weet het nooit!
Misschien is dit wel Doornroosje.
Locomotiefje, liefje... open je ogen...!

Hoog aan de hemel staat de zon.
'Hé!' roepen ze. 'Ho!', 'Wacht eens even!' en 'Sta stil!'.
Maar wij vertrekken en horen niets en niemand meer.

LOCOMOTIVE

There's a locomotive standing in a siding,
consumed by rust, overgrown with thistles.

When it rains, she cries, brown tears.

I walk alongside her, touch her,
stroke her,
say something to her, something encouraging,
climb up onto the remains of a footboard.

A clock strikes in the distance.
Perhaps I am a prince. You never know!
Perhaps this could just be Sleeping Beauty.
Little luvvy loco... open your eyes...!

The sun is high in the sky.
'Hey!' they call out. 'Ho!', 'Wait a moment!' and 'Stop!'
But we move off and hear nothing and no one any more.

Noli Me Tangere

Een vers is ballast. Zorg dat het vergaat.
Je kunt het slopen als je op het laatst
Een bom onder het deel dat er al staat,
Een landmijn in de laatste regel, plaatst.

Steek nu de lont vast aan. Een vrome wens.
Er is geen bom. Je bent gedwongen om
Je vers te vullen tot de verste grens.
Pas na een slalom stoot het op de bom.

Waarom schei je er, op dit punt beland,
Dan niet mee uit? Raak het niet langer aan.
Hier kan het nog. Maar verder gaat je hand.
Een vers moet rond zijn om niet te bestaan.

Noli Me Tangere

Verse is just ballast. Make it disappear.
You can demolish it if by some code
You cause a bomb (beneath the part that's there)
Or landmine (in the last line) to explode.

Make sure you light the fuse. A pious hope.
There is no bomb. Yet you're obliged, yes, come
What may, to swell the verse to its full scope.
Only beyond a slalom lurks the bomb.

At such a point, why do you not resist,
Stop fiddling with it, let it go, desist?
The cord is cut. Yet still you would persist.
A poem must be round to not exist.

GINDER

Ik zoek een dorp.
En daarin een huis. En daarin een
kamer, waarin een bed, waarin een vrouw.
En in die vrouw een schoot.

Buiten maakt de rivier zich breed
om ver te gaan, de zilvergeschubde,
vissenhebbende, botendragende,
zeezoekende, hierblijvende.

Zo zoekt een vergelijking
een gedicht voor een nacht,
een man een vrouw
een leeslint een vouw.
Nacht klapt het boek dicht.

HERMAN DE CONINCK 1944–1997

YONDER

I seek a village.
And in it a house. And in it a
room, in which there's a bed, in which there's a woman.
And in that woman a womb.

Outside the window the river swells
for a long journey, the silver-scaled,
fish-holding, boat-bearing,
sea-seeking, here-staying one.

Thus a simile seeks
a poem for the night,
a man a woman,
a bookmark a fold.
Night shuts the book.

Blues On Tuesday

Geen geld.
Geen vuur.
Geen speed.

Geen krant.
Geen wonder.
Geen weed.

Geen brood.
Geen tijd.
Geen weet.

Geen klote.
Geen donder.
Geen reet.

BLUES ON TUESDAY

No cash.
No light.
No speed.

No paper.
No wonder.
No weed.

No bread.
No time.
No idea.

No shit.
No damn.
No gear.

Verzoek Aan De Schilder

Mijn arsenaal van klank en taal
bestaat in tijd. Zij niet. Ik vraag

uw hulp. Als ik haar met mijn warme
hand, zo zwaar van bloed, wil raken

is er niets. U heeft een vlak met veertien
kleuren, een penseel van vossenhaar –

streel haar te voorschijn, groene schaduw
bij haar oor en in haar hals een zweem

van oud ivoor. Maak haar een plaats
in vezels van uw doek. Roep mij

dan binnen. U staart uit het raam.
Ik blijf op anderhalve meter staan.

Zij kijkt mij aan.

Plea To The Artist

My solid ground of tongue and sound
is time-bound. Not so she. I ask

your help. When with my warm
hand's blood-filled weight I'd touch her

nothing's there. Your palette's fourteen
colours, your brush of fox's hair –

caress her forth now, at her ear
green shadow and her neck a trace

of yellow ivory. Find her a place
in your canvas threads. Then call

me in. You're at the window staring.
I stand five feet away and see.

She looks at me.

NAZOMER

Zes blaren vielen hier
in een kleine weide liefelijk.
De aarde is jarig, de wind zoek.

In de rookblauwe oktoberlucht
hoor je het gefluit van hanen,
tuinhekjes en losse tanden.

Zes blaren tuimelden neer.
Met prijzen vereerd, in functies
gekozen, op posten benoemd.

FRANK KOENEGRACHT 1945–

Late Summer

Six leaves fell here
in a small meadow sweetly.
It's earth's birthday, the wind's gone.

In the smoke-blue October air
you hear the singing of cocks,
garden gates and loose teeth.

Six leaves came tumbling down.
Fêted with prizes, elected to
offices, appointed to posts.

DE RIVIER

Het lage vul ik met voorbijgaan
op en ik sleep door stad en land
verleden mee dat in mijn diepte

moet bezinken. Of ik nu dunner word of
zwel, ik slijp en slijt de binnenkanten
van m'n vel; mijn bedding ben ik

niet en wel. Voor links
en rechts heb ik geen oog, loom
drijvend op m'n onderstroom, de armen
zijwaarts soms gestrekt waardoor ik

nog meer grond betrek, verdrink ik
in het eigen ik. Niet dat ik
in mijzelf verstik, het hoge
vind ik daar en ook het slik.

HESTER KNIBBE 1946–

The River

I fill what is low-lying with my passing
and drag along with me through town and country
a past that has to settle

in my depths. No matter if I shrink
or swell, I wear and tear the inside
of my skin; my bed I'm

not and yet I am. I have no eye
for left and right: drifting slowly
on my undertow, my arms at times
outstretched, so that I

take in yet more ground, I drown
in my own me. Not that I
stifle in myself, heaven
I find there and also sludge.

Zeg Aan De Kinderen Dat Wij Niet Deugen

Zeg aan de kinderen dat wij niet deugen.
Zij moeten de mestkuil betalen, de beerput
Die wij in ons wolkenveld dolven, zij moeten
De hemelriolen ruimen, die stortplaats
Van stront in azuur waar de Ouden van zongen.

Mijn erfzonde heeft al hun zonnen verdonkeremaand.

Ons licht was vrijgevig. Wij hebben het smerig
Achtergelaten, er valt hier geen ster meer
Te zien in de straten, wij worden elektrisch
Verblind. Ons verstand sprong een gat in de lucht.
En doodgaan is soms een verademing straks.

LEONARD NOLENS 1947–

TELL THE CHILDREN WE'RE NO GOOD

Tell the children we're no good.
They must pay for the dung pit, the cesspool
That we dug in our bank of clouds, they must
Clear out the heavenly sewers, that dump filled
With shit in azure the Ancients sang of.

My primal sin has eclipsed all their suns.

Our light was bountiful once. We left it
Polluted: there isn't a star
To be seen in the streets, we're being electrically
Dazzled. Our minds jumped over the moon.
And the prospect of death sometimes seems a relief.

TOT GOD

God allemachtig, je kan me gestolen worden.
'k Heb jou niet lief en evenmin bemin ik het woord,
het vlees geworden, ferm gekneed en gaargestoofd
gehakt der schone poëzij. Al wat zich waarheid waant
en wil aanbeden, zal ik weerspreken

tot mijn tong verdroogt. Want ik ben dichter,
timmer gaten dicht en kieren, hamer schotten
tegen blikseminslag van het lot, sla spijkers
waar jouw donder dreigt, en vloek het gluipen
van de gifslang die jij zendt, o god.

Ik zal er staan, van aangezicht tot aangezicht
wanneer je duistre spiegel breekt; maar wel als David
met zijn slingersteen. Zolang ik duur, hoed ik
mijn hart, mijn wankel fort aan het ravijn dat jij
zo wonder schept – door slagen van je hand.

Ik baken wereld af, verweer me tegen overmacht
en roverlust: jij rooft gestaag de lieve levens
van wie mij lief zijn en met wie ik delen mag
de razernij om afscheid dat jij ons proeven doet
al in de eerste kus – jouw dood, jouw as, jouw roet.

To God

God almighty, I'd be well shot of you.
I love you not, nor do I love the word,
the now made flesh, well-kneaded, tender-simmered
meatball of fair poetry. All that would claim to truth
and fain be worshipped I'll refute

until my tongue be parched. For I'm a wordwright,
I work holes and fissures tight, hammer bulkheads
against fate's lightning strikes, sink nails
where your thunder threatens, and curse the wiles
of the deadly serpent that you send, oh God.

I shall stand there, face to face
when your dark mirror breaks; but as David
with his slingstone. As long as I last I'll protect
my heart, the shaky stronghold at the ravine you are
so wondrously creating – by scoops of your hand.

I mark off world, resist all higher power
and thieving urge: you filch the dear lives constantly
of all those dear to me and those with whom I like to share
the rage at leaving, the taste of which you've put
way back in the first kiss – your death, your ash, your soot.

SOLVE ET COAGULA

Toen je die bloedneus had weet je
nog wel, dat het niet meer ophield,
je zat bij de wasbak, hoofd voorovergevouwen,
'loop ik nou helemaal leeg?' en ik zag je daar zitten,

het was alsof ik je nooit meer
zou durven aanraken, of je meteen zou op-
lossen in de werkelijkheid als goud
in koningswater als ik je ook maar het minste
beetje zou aaien;

natuurlijk moest je nog lang niet
dood, dat wist ik best, maar hij die de liedjes
zingt voor de hazen en beren waarin hij vertelt
hoe hij ze heeft geschoten, was juist begonnen
het jouwe te maken, ik kon het
horen in mijn hoofd, *pieng*,
pong, de eerste,
voorzichtige tonen.

Solve Et Coagula

When you had that nose-bleed remember
the one that just wouldn't stop,
you sat head down over the basin
'will I bleed empty now?' and I looked at you there,

it was as if I never more would
dare touch you again, as if you'd dis-
solve then and there into reality like
gold in aqua regia had I but stroked
you the slightest;

of course you hadn't got to die for
ages, I knew that full well, but he who sings to
the hares and the bears the songs where
he tells how he shot them had now just
started on yours, I could hear it
inside my head *pling*,
plong, the opening
tentative notes.

Oud Vergaderzaaltje

Op de aaneengeschoven tafels
staat een dienblad met kopjes

een glazen kom met pakjes melkpoeder
een glazen kom met pakjes suiker
en een doos met theezakjes

thermoskannen, kasten uit een ver verleden
een in onbruik rakende flap-over als

een schildersezel in het zuiden van Frankrijk
waar de lucht trilt van de warmte
zodat de cipressen lijken op gefilmde cipressen

leeg, golvend landschap met stenen muurtjes
en verlaten landhuizen

musea met oude suppoosten op klapstoelen en
succesvolle directeuren die
langslopen terwijl ze naar de schilderijen kijken

auto's op parkeerterreinen
schoolbussen met schoolkinderen.

MARTIN REINTS 1950–

OLD MEETING ROOM

On the pushed-together tables
stands a tray with cups

a glass bowl with sachets of milk-powder
a glass bowl with sachets of sugar
and a packet of tea-bags

thermos flasks, cabinets from a distant past
a flap-over fallen into disuse like

an easel in the south of France
where the air shimmers with the heat
so that the cypresses look like filmed cypresses

an empty, undulating landscape with stone walls
and desolate country cottages

museums with old attendants on folding chairs and
successful directors who
walk past while looking at the paintings

cars in car parks
school buses with schoolchildren.

Marsyas

Nadat de telefoon met schuim op de hoorn
en nog stuipend onder verre lippen
als een beledigde afluisteraar was gaan liggen
begon de hele weigering van voren af aan.

Hij ging dus, grimassen makend, voor de gebroken
spiegel staan, maakte zijn haren nat en
kamde ze strak achterover, deed crème op
het blauwe litteken, van mond tot oren.

Jasje, das, een minieme sjaal in passend grijs
bij dit driedelig pak van zacht geweven ijs.
En toen hij in de diepe snede zag dat alles
er nog was, begon hij met de overjas.

Hij scheurde hem eerst overlangs, dan dwars,
en liet de repen op een hoop elkaar betasten;
bond met de das het jasje en het hemd,
en met de broekriem nog zijn adem en zijn stem.

Hij schoor oksels, liezen, oren; vulde de waskom
met zijn afgestroopte huid. Zo kleedde hij
zich tweemaal uit, en bleef toen rillend
bij de spiegel en het neon.

Zijn schitterend omhulsel dreef in vlokken
op van bloed doordesemd water; het schuim
dat op zijn lippen stond, maakte zijn rauwe
ledematen jong, totdat zijn innerlijk zich

Marsyas

After the telephone, foaming at the mouthpiece
and still in spasm under distant lips
had lain down again like an affronted eavesdropper
the whole refusal began again from square one.

So, grimacing, he went over to the broken
mirror, wetted his hair and
combed it straight back, put cream
on the blue scar, from mouth to ears.

Jacket, tie, a minimal scarf in matching grey
with this three-piece suit of soft woven ice.
And when he saw in that deep gash that everything
was still there, he started on the overcoat.

First he tore it lengthways, then across,
and let the strips grope each other in a heap;
bound the jacket and shirt with the tie,
and with the belt his breath and voice.

He shaved armpits, groins, ears; filled the washbasin
with his stripped-off skin. This way he
undressed twice, and was left shivering
in the mirror and the neon.

His brilliant shell floated in flakes
on blood-leavened water; the foam
on his lips, made his raw
limbs young, until his inner self

huiverend en naamloos door de omtrek van
het uit zijn oevers tredend lichaam wrong. Toen stormden
alle stemmen op hem af, die
hem verwachtten op het feest, waar hij
niet was geweest.

struggled shivering and nameless through
the bounds of his overflowing body.
Then all the voices came charging towards him that
were expecting him at the party, where
he hadn't appeared.

Op De Hoge

Liep augustus op zijn einde,
sloot de badmeester de hokjes af,
fietste neuriënd september in.

Niemand was er dan ook bij
dat ik de plank betrad. Ik was
geblinddoekt als een deserteur.

Dit zijn de stappen bang bang bang.
In het Bosbad op de hoge
zweet men het peentje bangverlang.

De zon stond even laag als ik en stond
op punt van zakken in de grond.
Wie mij naar boven had gebracht?

Ach mijn lief. En ik wist: morgen
word ik wakker maar ontkomen
kan ik niet. Uit de schoonspringdroom

ontwaakt men met de schoonspringdroom.
Ik wist: ik maak ze nu dan dus.
De aanstalten. Ik sta precies

zo hoog als nodig om bevreesd te zijn.
Dit is de toegedachte afstand tot
het lussenwevend water doopselzacht.

Het heeft me altijd opgewacht –
maar waarom vrees ik dan ineens het bad
alsof het heel snel leeggelopen is?

WILLEM JAN OTTEN 1951–

ON THE HIGH BOARD

With August drawing to a close,
the bath attendant locked the cubicles,
biked whistling off into September.

So no one was around when I
stepped out onto the board. I was
blindfolded like a deserter.

These are the steps up dread tread dread.
On the high board of the Forest Baths
one flirts with the frisson of fear.

The sun was just as low as I and was
about to slowly sink into the ground.
Who had transported me aloft?

Oh dear love. And I knew: tomorrow
I will wake but no escape for me is
possible. From the springboard-dream

one wakes up with the springboard-dream.
I knew: I'm going to do it then.
The preparations. I stand precisely

at the height required to feel afraid.
This is the right intended distance to
the loop-looming water, baptismal-soft.

It's always lain in wait for me –
so why abruptly do I fear the pool
as if it rapidly had drained away?

Dat zo ik sprong – ik wil, ik wil –
ik vallen zou en niets mij ving?

That if I dived – I will, I will –
I was to fall and nothing catch me?

Er Woonde Op De Aarde

Er woonde op de aarde
een vrouw van honderd jaar
die veel te veel bewaarde,
ik weet alleen niet waar.

Wat iemand had vergeten,
wat iemand niet meer zag,
wat bijna was versleten,
wat in een laatje lag.

Wat in antieke kasten
en diepe putten bleef,
wat nergens meer in paste,
wat schonkig was en scheef.

En niet als in de dromen
en elke dag te moe,
ze heeft het meegenomen,
ik weet niet waar naartoe.

A Woman Who Was Old As Old

A woman who was old as old,
a hundred years or more,
kept far too much, so I've been told,
though where I'm not quite sure.

Those things that someone now forgot,
those things that no one saw,
those things worn out as like as not,
or things in some old drawer.

Those things deep in some antique chest
or in some hidden well,
those things that stuck out from the rest,
all bones or hard to tell.

Not like those found in secret dreams
and those too tired to care,
she's taken them away, it seems,
though I'm not sure quite where.

Een Goed Mens Is Iets Heel Eenvoudigs

Een goed mens is iets heel eenvoudigs,
maar laat je hem vallen, dan kun je hem weggooien.
Als het verband eruit is, krijgen
de knapste vaklui dat er nooit meer in.
Je kunt hem weggooien, hij is niets meer waard.

Koeien worden als ze gedwongen
elkaars merg en kop hebben gedronken
bij duizenden over de kling gejaagd:
want er mocht eens één zo'n kostbaar, uniek...!

Een mens is echter zo vervangbaar als een gloeilamp.
Draai in de fitting van een kapot goed mens
een nieuw goed mens en je hebt licht.

Ook een goed gedicht is eenvoudig.

Nooitvanzijnlangzalhijleven

Ik houd een onderdeel over.

A Good Person Is Something Quite Simple

A good person is something quite simple,
but if you drop him, you can just as well throw him away.
Once the connection's lost, not even
the best technicians can ever put it back in.
You can throw him away, he's not worth anything any more.

Cows when they have forcibly drunk
each other's marrow and head
are put to the sword by the thousand:
the very thought that such a precious, unique...!

A human being however is as replaceable as a light-bulb.
Screw a new good person into the fitting
of a burnt-out good person and you have light.

A good poem is also simple.

Noneofthatyourverygoodhealth

I'm left with an extra bit.

Xxiv

Aan de ene kant staat het ding.
Aan de andere kant staat het mysterie.
Meer van het ding en het mysterie weet ik niet.

Hoe in naam van wat dan ook,
Hoe kan ik er meer van weten?
En dit weten is een klein weten, voeg ik er aan toe,
Een klein idee hoogstens, klein
In zijn gevolgen voor de tijd.

Als aan de ene kant staat het ding
En aan de andere kant het mysterie,
Is de wereld duidelijk.

De straat is de straat waarin ik vrienden tegenkom,
De bloemen bloeien zoals zij moeten bloeien, met bloesems,
De wind waait wanneer zij wil,
En het gebrek aan meer weten
Dan dat aan de ene kant staat het ding
En aan de andere kant het mysterie
Is mij een onuitputtelijke bron van vreugde.

Xxiv

On the one hand there's the thing.
On the other hand there's the mystery.
More about the thing and the mystery I do not know.

How in the name of whatever,
How can I know anything more about them?
And this knowledge is small knowledge, I would add,
A small idea at most, small
In its consequences for time.

If on the one hand there's the thing
And on the other hand the mystery,
The world is explicit.

The street is the street where I come across friends,
The flowers bloom as they must bloom, with blossoms,
The wind blows wherever it wishes,
And the lack of more knowledge
Than that on the one hand there's the thing
And on the other hand the mystery
Is to me an inexhaustible source of joy.

Bodemonderzoek

Dit is oude grond, de tijd is hier vertraagd,
al zijn momenten liggen hier voorbij
te wezen, de chaos van eeuwen, gestapeld,
gelaagd en tot orde geraakt. Wij lezen

bijvoorbeeld een vloer in het hart van de stad
ver onder het maaiveld, in de muren eromheen
de gekantelde tussenhaakjes van gewelven,
een deuropening gedicht met de liggende

denkstreepjes van stenen – iemand heeft
hier op schoenen die nooit zijn gevonden
in de vochtige schemer van zijn kelder
gestaan op plavuizen waar niemand bij stilstond

en dacht: die deur moet weg. Want hij had tijd,
het was voortdurend nu. Hij bouwde en
veranderde bouwsels, zijn heden was eeuwig
en er was zoveel om te willen, vast te houden.

Soil Survey

This is ancient ground, time is slowed right down,
here all of its moments lie in being
past, the chaos of centuries, stacked,
stratified and brought to order. We read

for example a floor in the heart of the city
far below ground level, in the surrounding walls
the toppled brackets of vaults,
a door opening blocked with the reclining

dashes of stones – someone has stood
here on shoes that have never been found
in the dank twilight of his cellar
on flagstones that made no one stop

and thought: that door must go. For he had time,
it was continuously now. He built and
altered buildings, his present was eternal
and there was so much to want, to hold on to.

OOK DE VISSEN

Zou je de Haagse Hofvijver overeind zetten
rechtstandig als een majestueuze wand van water
om het licht de diepte te laten doorstralen
om de stad een doorzichtige spiegel te bieden

een oudgouden glans zou over de huizen strijken
en iemand roept als eerste 'kijk' en wijst
toeterend komt het hele verkeer tot stilstand
abrupt worden alle vergaderingen opgeschort
en de straten vullen zich met ogen en geroezemoes

een vorstelijk banket, jagers in een herfstbos
zegels en paperassen, gesluierde naakte vrouwen
iedereen ziet in de vijverwand iets anders
maar allemaal blikken ze diep in de tijd terug

En eindelijk kunnen de hofvissen ook eens
over de schubbenhuid van de daken uitkijken
naar de glinsterende torens en ijspaleizen
de bomen bij de duinen, het gele strandzand

'kijk', stoten de vissen elkaar aan, 'dat zilvergrijze
dat schitterende schuimende, woelende weidse
dat zich daar uitstrekt tot aan de einder en verder
dat is nou de zee, ja dat daar is de zee'

The Fish Too

If you stood the Royal Pond in The Hague on end
upright like a majestic wall of water
to let the light irradiate the depths
to hand the city a transparent mirror

an old-gold sheen would brush the houses
and someone would be first to cry 'look' and point
the traffic all comes hooting to a halt
all meetings are abruptly adjourned
and the streets are filled with eyes and hubbub

a princely banquet, hunters in an autumn wood
seals and documents, veiled naked women
everyone sees something different in the pond wall
but all of them look deep back into time

And finally the royal fish can also
look out over the scaly skin of roofs
at the glittering towers and ice palaces
the trees by the dunes, the yellow beach sand

'look', the fish nudge each other, 'that silver-grey
that shimmering foaming, churning vast thing
that stretches there to the horizon and beyond
that's the sea then, yes that there's the sea'

Showen En Trippen

Er is zielsveel geluk nodig in deze jurk met vertedering
    naar buren
te kijken die rond middernacht hun afvalzak in een
    container doen.

Er is zielsveel geluk nodig in deze jurk een taxi aan te
    houden die onwillig is
je tot buiten de stad te rijden waar loofwoud staat dat zich
    voortplant.

Er is zielsveel geluk nodig deze jurk dronken en klaarwakker
    naar een show
te brengen, blind een deur te vinden waardoor je het toneel
    verlaat.

Er is zielsveel geluk nodig in deze jurk iets te slikken, een
    ballonvaart
te maken en op het mozaïek van je land neer te kijken als
    een slome astronaut.

Er is zielsveel geluk nodig in stralend weer voorzichtig te
    verongelukken.
Stemmen schreeuwen zeggen wade in plaats van jurk.

Shows And Trips

It needs oceans of happiness to watch tenderly in this
    dress
as around midnight neighbours put their rubbish bag into
    a Grundon.

It needs oceans of happiness in this dress to hail a taxi that
    is unwilling
to drive you out of town to where deciduous woods are
    reproducing.

It needs oceans of happiness to take this dress drunk and
    wide awake to a show,
blindly find a door through which you leave the stage.

It needs oceans of happiness to swallow something in this
    dress, take a balloon
trip and look down at the mosaic of our country, like a
    befuddled astronaut.

It needs oceans of happiness to have another careful
    accident in glorious weather.
Voices scream say shroud instead of dress.

DE NIEUWE VIS

Al bij opserveren van het exemplaar
staken belendende tafels het graven
van verdere greppels in de kastanjepuree,

het afplaggen van de verruigde salades
stagneert, wijnen talmen in geheven glazen:
de gebruikelijke gezelligheid uit zee

is deze vis niet. Een openbaring,
opgehaald uit wateren van aanvang
lijkt ze. Al ontbraken kop en staartvin,

ervaren vissers verbeten hun tranen
bij het zien van de borsten, de aanzet
tot ledematen. Hoeveel soorten moesten

vergaan voor deze ongeëvenaarde? Of
zijn eruit ontstaan? Maar het ogenblik
van nuttigen is daar. Ongewis moment:

de kok stond voor een culinair raadsel.
Hoe bereid je wat niet eerder bereid is
en ogenschijnlijk in zichzelf volmaakt?

Pocheren, braden, marineren? Overbodig,
een belediging. En daarna? Hou je het
simpel met zeewier en mootjes op toast

of vraagt dit om een complexe brandade
voor de meereisende maag? Rauw, ongesneden
werd het, met struisvogelei en slobeendrollade.

ERIK MENKVELD 1959–2014

The New Fish

Already when the specimen is being served
adjoining tables stop the digging
of further trenches in the chestnut purée,

the spading of curled-up lettuce leaves
stagnates, wines linger in lifted glasses:
this fish is not the convivial fare

from the deep. A revelation,
hauled it would seem from primordial
waters. Though head and tail-fin gone,

seasoned fishermen blinked back their tears
at the sight of breasts, the rudiments
of limbs. How many species had had to

perish for this peerless creature? Or
in it had their origin? But the time
has come for consumption. Uncertain moment:

the chef was faced with a culinary enigma.
How to prepare what's never been prepared
and in itself is seemingly complete?

Poach, braise or marinate? Superfluous,
an insult. And what then? Do you keep things
simple with seaweed and slivers on toast

or does this call for a complex brandade
for the more demanding stomach? Raw, unsliced
it became, with ostrich egg and shoveller roulade.

Zelfs het plonzend ijsklontenwater
onderbreekt zich nu op het uitstroompunt.
Daar steekt de uitverkoren eerste eter

de eerste hap in zijn mond. Hij kauwt
in stilte en ongekende overgave. Begint
dan ijselijke kreten te slaken. Uit afkeer

of extase? Minutenlang danst hij rond
en bedaart tot verbijsterd staren. Zelfs
na de soesjes kan hij er niet over praten.

Even the sploshing ice-cube water
halts at the point of pouring.
Then the first elected eater places

the first forkful in his mouth. He chews
in silence and unparalleled abandonment. Then
starts to utter ghastly screams. Revulsion,

ecstasy perhaps? He dances round for minutes,
subsiding into baffled staring. Even
after the babas he can't speak about it.

OP HET JODENKERKHOF

liggen vele stenen omgegooid. Hun ligging
lijkt me niet lukraak, en ook hun val is zo
te zien niet door de zwaartekracht, maar door
een macht veroorzaakt die een reden heeft.

Zodat elke steen of zerk daar met een
doel – een ziel – ligt neergesmakt en op de
bühne van het kerkhof wacht totdat er
iemand die begrijpt uit de coulissen komt.

Maar wat doe ik dan hier? Niet één van deze
stenen lichamen beweegt, geen stem wordt
hoorbaar door hun grijze omtrek heen.
Altijd staan we als vreemden naast

elkaar. Van hen naar mij reikt geen gebaar
dat lang genoeg kan zijn.

ERIK SPINOY 1960–

At The Jewish Cemetery

many of the stones lie overturned. Their lie
does not seem random to me, nor their fall
as being caused by gravity, but rather by
a power that has an underlying reason.

So that each slab or tombstone there lies
thwacked down with a purpose – a soul – and waits
on the bühne of the cemetery till someone
who comprehends comes in from the wings.

But what then am I doing here? None of these
stone bodies moves at all, no voice is to
be heard that pierces their grey outlines.
We always stand as strangers next to one

another. From them to me no gesture reaches out
that can be long enough.

ZACHTE HUID

Kinderen maken rustig.
Zij hebben een zachte huid.
Zij slapen op je graf.
Zij hebben grote ogen.
Zij kijken rustiger.
Zij slapen naast elkaar.
Je geeft elk kind een dood dier
om te leren in te slapen met een dier in zijn hand,
gezicht tegen gezicht gedrukt.
Als het dier al zijn haren verloren heeft
neem je het kind het dier af en leg je 's nachts
een levend dier naast zijn opgerold lichaam.

NACHOEM M. WIJNBERG 1961–

SOFT SKIN

Children have a calming effect.
They have a soft skin.
They sleep on your grave.
They have big eyes.
They look more calmly.
They sleep next to each other.
You give each child a dead animal
to teach it to fall asleep holding onto an animal,
face pressed against face.
When the animal has lost all its hair
you take the animal away from the child and place
at night a living animal beside its curled-up body.

GEEN REVOLVER

Voor Bert Schierbeek

Het regent, de laatste bloemen
laten los, maar de mensen bloeien.

Hölderlin leest even helder,
verduistert dan; gordijnen worden

dichtgetrokken overdag. Deuren sluiten
zonder sleutelgat. Het regent hard.

Toch: wezens denken dat de wereld
beter wordt, vrouwen trekken lippenstift

en geen revolver. Vrouwen baden kinderen,
maar de hemel maakt hun water zwart.

Toch: tijd rolt zich uit om mensen langer
tijd te geven en nu zal Hölderlin wat gniffelen

om de laatste peren. Maar hij heeft ongelijk:
het is zijn waanzin die naar de pijpen danst van as.

Het regent, de laatste bloemen
strooien kindjes op de oude aarde.

En Hölderlin buigt zich over zijn gedicht,
schrapt wat woorden, drinkt en bidt.

No Revolver

For Bert Schierbeek

It's raining, the last of the flowers are
letting go, but people are blooming.

Hölderlin briefly reads clearly
then clouds over: curtains are shut

during the daytime. Doors close
without a keyhole. It's raining hard.

And yet: humans believe that the world is
getting better, women draw a lipstick

and no revolver. Women bathe children,
but the sky turns their water black.

And yet: time unreels to give people
extra time and now Hölderlin will chuckle a bit

about the last pears. Although he's mistaken:
it is his madness dancing to ashes' tune.

It's raining, the last flowers are
strewing children on the old earth.

And Hölderlin pores over his poem,
scratches some words, drinks and prays.

BRIEF ACHTENTWINTIG
(Hadewijch-variatie)

Als ik zwijg kan ik u horen. Wat ik hoor
legt mij het zwijgen op. Wat ik verzwijgen moet

hoor ik met mijn ziel vol tanden aan.
Als ik u uitspreek scheuren de talen mij open

– dus ik zwijg en ik slaap
in het voorhoofd van uw nacht.

Blijf, trek het laken der firmamenten
niet van mij af. Laat uw naakte hemel

en diens hemisferen als een dakloos
raadsel op mijn ogen rusten.

Leg een vinger op mijn lippen Liefste.
Uit één vinger valt men niet.

ERWIN MORTIER 1965–

LETTER TWENTY-EIGHT
(Hadewijch variation)

Should I stay silent I can hear you. What I hear
silence imposes on me. What I must keep silent

I listen to my soul tongue-tied.
When I speak your name, languages tear me open

– so I clam shut and sleep
in the temple of your night.

Bide, do not snatch from me the sheet of
all the firmament. Let your naked heaven

and its hemispheres rest on my eyes
like a roofless enigma.

Place a finger on my lips Beloved.
From one finger one can't fall.

Zwembad Den Dolder

Er zijn gevoelens die fascistisch zijn.
De vader die niet weet waarom hij slaat,
de zoon die half verstikt in foto's krast.

De mooiste idioot die ik ooit zag
lag op zijn rug een heel heelal te zijn.
Geen vader kreeg ooit greep op deze pees

die als een kosmonaut het bad door dreef,
geen moeder stookte in zijn vissenkom.
En wit en scheef en wijs zwom hij. Hij zwom.

SWIMMING POOL DEN DOLDER*

There are emotions of a fascist kind.
The father who hits out but can't tell why,
the son half-choked who scratches photos through.

The loveliest idiot I ever saw
lay on his back, a total universe.
No father got to grasp this basket case

that drifted through the pool like one in space,
no mother poked his bowl of fish around.
And skewed and pale and wise he swam. Swam sound.

* Den Dolder clinic

HET RAAM MAAKT EEN KIER

Het raam maakt een kier
en de tafel tot hier
breekt
op slag

en de tafel is niet bij het raam
maar hier naast me gaan staan
aan de voet van de tafel
valt het kleed van de tafel

in het licht van het raam
buigt het blad een armlengte
breekt een elleboog een reep
in de lade: kruimels, paperclips

het stuk karton dat de tafel recht
en het raam open houdt

een schuivend vierkant over de tafel
raakt aan een stuk de grond.

The Window Opens a Crack

The window opens a crack
and the table to here
breaks
at once

and the table's not by the window
but has moved next to me here
at the foot of the table
the cloth falls off the table

in the light of the window
the light bends an arm's length
a bar breaks at the elbow
in the drawer: crumbs, paperclips

the cardboard wedge that keeps the table
straight and the window open

a shifting square over the table
touches the ground in one piece.

Voor De Liefste Onbekende

Wie van ons twee heeft de ander bedacht? – Paul Eluard

Wat ben ik blij dat ik je nog niet ken.
Ik dank de sterren en de maan
dat iedereen die komt en gaat
de diepste sporen achterlaat, behalve jij,
dat jij mijn deuren, dicht of open,
steeds voorbijgelopen bent.

Het is maar goed dat je me niet herkent.
Kussen onder straatlantaarns
en samen dwalen door de regen,
wéér verliefd zijn, wéér verliezen,
bijna sterven van verdriet –
dat hoeft nu allemaal nog niet.

Ik ben nog niet aan ons gehecht.
Ik kijk bepaald niet naar je uit.
Neem de tijd, als je dat wilt.
Wacht een maand, een jaar,
de eeuwigheid en één seconde meer –
maar kom, voor ik mijn ogen sluit.

FOR THE BELOVED STRANGER

'Which of us dreamed up the other?' – Paul Eluard

How glad I am I don't yet know your name,
I thank the sun and thank the moon
that everyone who comes and goes
leaves the deepest traces, but you,
that when my doors were open or shut
you always passed them by.

It's just as well that you don't know my face.
Kissing and cuddling under street lamps' light,
wandering together through the rain,
in love once more, losers once more,
almost dying with the pain –
none of that's yet needed once again.

I'm not yet attached to us.
I'm not expecting you in any guise.
Take your time, if you prefer.
Wait a month, a year,
eternity and one second more –
but come, before I close my eyes.

DE SNEEUWKONINGIN

Kai heeft scherven in zijn ogen.
Zijn hart is een blok ijs. Dus denkt hij
dat hij bij mij moet zijn,
aan deze kou genoeg heeft. Bevroren vijvers,

blauw paleis reusachtig om hem heen
en niemand hier dan ik,
dan hij, dan ijs.
Wie zegt dat je warm moet zijn?

Blijf hier Kai. Hier bederf je niet.
Je bent bevroren, dat is alles.
Dat is toch beter dan verloren
aan de liefde?

Zijn meisje zoekt hem, ik hoor haar,
ze vraagt aan de rozen of hij dood is.
'Nee,' zeggen de rozen, 'hij is niet dood,
alles wat dood is, is onder de aarde,
wij hebben hem daar niet gezien.'

Zijn meisje leent een rendier van een roversdochter,
ze is al bijna hier, Kai, luister niet naar haar,
smelt niet, bedenk wat je zult missen als je weggaat!
Alle ruimte is van jou en alle kou

en al het ijskoud blauw dat je hier ziet
en alle sterren zijn hier altijd zichtbaar.
En ik zie jouw gezicht zo graag,
bevroren witte waterlelie.

The Snow Queen

Kay has splinters in his eyes.
His heart's a block of ice. Thus he believes
he has to be with me,
this cold's sufficient. Ponds frozen,

blue palace gigantic all around him
and no one here but me,
than him, than ice.
Who says you have to be warm?

Stay here Kay. Here you'll not decay.
You are just frozen, nothing more.
That's better surely than being
lost to love?

His girl is seeking him, I hear her,
she's asking the roses if he's dead.
'No,' say the roses, 'he's not dead,
all that is dead is under the ground,
and none of us have seen him down there.'

His girl is borrowing a reindeer from a robber maiden,
she'll be here very soon, Kay, do not listen to her,
don't melt, just think of what you'll miss if you should leave!
All space is yours, likewise all cold

and all the ice-cold blue you can see here
and all the stars are always visible.
And I so like to see your face,
frozen white water lily.

Het is te laat.
Hij ziet haar al.
Hij is al niet meer hier.

Het moest maar eens gaan sneeuwen.

It is too late.
He has already seen her.
He is no longer here.

It'd better start snowing soon.

OOK WIJ, TITAANTJES

We hadden geen benul van hoe het liep.
We deden dingen omdat je dingen doet.
We richtten daden aan en lazen soms een boek
om te vieren dat gedachten niet vergingen.

We gingen door omdat je verder moet
of bleven haken aan een onverwachte blik
omdat er blikken zijn waarmee iets wordt bedoeld,
vooral wanneer bedoeld was wat wij wilden.

We vingen aan en rondden ook wel af
maar wat in gang gezet was ging zijn eigen weg toch weer.
We maakten plannen, legden ons erbij neer
dat dingen gingen zoals ze niet waren voorvoeld.

We liepen af toen het eenmaal zo ver was
dat wat niet voorvoeld was onomkeerbaar bleek.
We lieten wat we hadden in de steek
en zochten naar wat ons verlaten had.

WE TOO, TINY TITANS

We had no clue what it was all about.
We did things just since things are what you do.
Performed our deeds and sometimes read a book
to celebrate that thoughts don't die on you.

We pushed ahead because you must go on
or stopped short at an unexpected look
for there are looks where meaning's clearly sent,
above all when we wanted what was meant.

We started and we rounded off it seemed
but what was set in motion followed its own path.
We made our plans, though all the while resigned
to things not going as we thought they might.

We just ran out when we had reached the stage
that unforeseen things could not be reversed.
All that we had we left there in the lurch
and searched for that which had abandoned us.

Daar Horen We Engelen Zingen

Niemand is in leven, een oude klacht. Je moet flink
    kauwen
en slikken, de geboden zijn taai. Gij zult niet liegen of
    stelen,
gij zult geen vreemde zijn, niet welkom heten en
    altijd kun je
je legitimeren. Zelfs hier, waar je ligt te verpieteren,
    ergens

in een uithoek van de wereld, waar machientjes blije
    geluiden
produceren, waar iedere siddering wordt gemeten en
    spiegels
reflecteren. Waar geen wind bij kan, geen natuurlijk
    licht, je
hebt de elementen lief. Wind erodeert, water doet
    verweren.

Water, bevroren, is niet transparant maar grijswit,
    inktzwart
wanneer het geweld pleegt en daar zit je hartspier en
    daar zit
je lever. Je vermoordt nog eens iemand, wijst naar
    je hoofd:

'Ik ben een teken.' Je lacht, zigzagt verschrikkelijk,
    stromend
is water zonder genade maar soms wordt een rivier
    gehinderd
in zijn loop. Door hardere steenlagen, dwars in zijn
    bedding.

THERE WE HEAR ANGELS SINGING

Nobody is alive, an old complaint. You have to chew and
    swallow
hard, the commandments are tough. Thou shalt not lie
    nor steal,
thou shalt not be a stranger, nor be welcomed and must
    always be able
to identify yourself. Even here, where you pine away,
    somewhere

in a far corner of the world, where little machines make
    happy
sounds, where every tremor is registered and where
    mirrors
reflect. Where no wind can get through, no natural
    light, you
love the elements. Wind erodes, water causes
    weathering.

Water, frozen, is not transparent but greyish-white,
    ink-black
when committing violence and there is your heart muscle,
    there
your liver. You'll get to murder someone once, point to
    your head:

'I am a sign.' You laugh, zigzag most terribly,
    flowing
water is without mercy, but sometimes a river is
    impeded
in its course. By harder layers of rock, across the
    channel.

VATNAJÖKULL

Een zwarte fysiotherapeut op IJsland nodigde me uit
voor een wandeling. Hij keek naar mijn heupen

en ik zag een toekomst. Hij zei: 'Je houding is verkeerd.'
Schouders naar achter borst vooruit.

Ik sjokte door de sneeuw bleek als mijn omgeving
en hij bewoog zich magistraal in het wit.

Toen hij me de top van de Vatnajökull wees
kraakte de sneeuw onder mijn voeten.

De aardkorst scheurde tot ik rechtop
onder een ijskap stond. Zo kon ik net over het ijs

de wereld in kijken waar de fysiotherapeut
me op zijn knieën de hand reikte.

IJswater rond mijn voeten klatert in een diepte
waar ik met een enkele stap in kan verdwijnen.

Het is wit in mijn hoofd. Kan iemand me details geven?
Ik sta in het midden van een verbijsterd heelal.

VATNAJÖKULL

A black physiotherapist in Iceland invited me out
for a walk. He looked at my hips

and I saw a future. He said: 'Your posture is wrong.'
Shoulders back, chest out.

I jolted through the snow pallid as my surroundings
and he moved majestically in the white.

When he showed me the top of the Vatnajökull
the snow scrunched under my feet.

The earth's crust tore until I was standing
upright under an ice cap. Then over the ice I was just able

to gaze into the world where the physiotherapist
on his knees stretched out a hand to me.

Ice water round my feet splatters into an abyss
into which with a single step I can disappear.

It is white inside my head. Can anyone give me details?
I'm standing in the middle of a baffled universe.

In Het Land Der Koningen*

ik leef in een land
waar de dierenvriend besluit
uit goedheid een andere mens neer te knallen

ik leef in een land
waar de vrome gelovige besluit
uit eerbied het mes in de ketter te planten

ik leef in een land
waar onze jongens uit gekkigheid soms
de conducteur in elkaar stampen

ik leef in een land
waar een keurige man, achtendertig, blond
de vrijheid neemt om door anderen heen te rammen

en in dit rood, rood schemerland
waar de grenzen totaal werden opgeheven
waar de mondigheid totterdood wordt beleden
en waar zestien miljoen koningen leven

daar ontstaat vanzelf een nieuwe orde
daar zal langs feestelijk afgezette lanen
een laatste koningin haar laatste onderdanen
als beesten overreden zien worden

* Vier jaar was Ramsey Nasr de Nederlandse Dichter des Vaderlands.
In deze periode gaf Nasr in zijn gedichten en opiniestukken zijn visie op
de actualiteit. Dit gedicht werd geschreven op de dag van de aanslag op
het Koninklijk Huis, gepleegd door de Nederlander Karst T., op 30 april
2009, Koninginnedag. Karst T. reed op volle snelheid met een Suzuki
Swift door een menigte, met als doelwit de bus waarmee de Koninklijke
Familie een rijtoer maakte. Zeven slachtoffers en de dader komen om.

RAMSEY NASR 1974–

In The Land Of Kings*

I live in a land
where the animal-lover decides
from sheer goodness to shoot a fellow man

I live in a land
where the righteous believer decides
from respect to plant the knife in the heretic

I live in a land
where our lads for the hell of it sometimes
kick the shit out of the train guard

I live in a land
where a smartly-dressed man, thirty-eight, blond,
takes the liberty of mowing down other people in his car

and in this red, red twilight land
where boundaries have been totally erased
where responsibility's professed ad nauseam
where sixteen million kings have been raised

a new order naturally starts
along festively cordoned-off lanes
a last queen will see her last subjects' remains
run over like animals' parts

* Ramsey Nasr was Poet Laureate of the Netherlands for four years.
During this time Nasr expressed his view of current affairs in his poems
and articles. This poem was written on 30 April 2009, the day of the
attack on the Royal Family by the Dutchman Karst T., and the Queen's
official birthday. Karst T. drove a Suzuki Swift at full speed through
a crowd of people, targeting the bus in which the Royal Family were
touring the area. Seven victims and the culprit himself were killed.

259

Na de moord op het populaire parlementslid Pim Fortuyn, en film-maker Theo van Gogh was dit de derde politieke aanslag in zeven jaar tijd. Dit gedicht verscheen op 1 mei 2009, op de voorpagina van het *NRC*.

After the murder of the popular MP Pim Fortuyn and that of filmmaker Theo van Gogh this was third violent political attack in the space of seven years. This poem appeared on 1 May 2009, on the front page of the daily *NRC/Handelsblad.*

Brandend Huis*

zij woont in een brandend huis
elke storm neemt een pan van het dak
het is koud haar tanden klapperen
buiten bedenkt iemand nieuwe verkeersregels
fietst verder een oude man
kranten om zijn lijf gebonden onder de kleren
zij loopt naar buiten met een mand vol was
zwarte lakens zwarte dekens zwarte sloop
ze ziet de velden branden ook
het heeft geen zin om buiten te zijn
liever terug naar de muren
de dansende vlammen op zijn portret
post valt ongevraagd door de deur
haalt knisperend de mat niet
haar kat springt bij haar op schoot
met een plantaardig streelverlangen
giet zij nog wat spiritus over de fotoalbums
veegt de as van haar bril en leest
en leest en leest

*Nederlandse vertaling, Dutch translation

Burning House

she lives in a burning house
every storm takes a tile from the roof
it is cold her teeth are chattering
outside someone makes up new traffic regulations
an old man goes on cycling
wrapped in newspapers under his clothing
she goes outside with a basket of washing
black sheets black blankets black pillowcase
she sees the fields burning too
it makes no sense to be outside
better to go back to the walls
the dancing flames on his portrait
post drops unasked for through the door
crackling fails to reach the mat
her cat jumps up onto her lap
with a plantlike desire to be stroked
she pours more meths over the photo albums
brushes ash from her specs and reads
and reads and reads

BAARNEND HÛS*

sy wennet yn in baarnend hûs
elke stoarm nimt in panne fan it dak
it is kâld har tosken klapperje
bûten betinkt ien nije ferkearsregels
fytst fierder in âld man
kranten om it liif bûn ûnder de klean
sy rint der út mei in koer fol wask
swarte lekkens swarte tekkens swart sloop
se sjocht de greiden baarne ek
it hat gjin doel en wês bûten
leaver werom nei de muorren
de dânsjende flammen op syn portret
post falt net frege troch de doar
hellet knisterjend de matte net
har kat springt by har op 'e skurte
mei in plantaardich streakferlet
jit sy noch wat spiritus oer de foto-albums
faget de jiske fan 'e bril en lêst
en lêst en lêst

*Origineel in het Fries, original poem in Frisian

TSEAD BRUINJA 1974–

Burning House

she lives in a burning house
every storm takes a tile from the roof
it is cold her teeth are chattering
outside someone makes up new traffic regulations
an old man goes on cycling
wrapped in newspapers under his clothing
she goes outside with a basket of washing
black sheets black blankets black pillowcase
she sees the fields burning too
it makes no sense to be outside
better to go back to the walls
the dancing flames on his portrait
post drops unasked for through the door
crackling fails to reach the mat
her cat jumps up onto her lap
with a plantlike desire to be stroked
she pours more meths over the photo albums
brushes ash from her specs and reads
and reads and reads

HARTKLOPPINGEN

Jij
    blond
        doorzichtig en beknopt
                        gezichtje
bla
    bladerde
        puberend

door de Actueel

lachte naar me
een keer
    of vijf

Bij alle zwermen Stem
    die mij belagen
        – mijn pooltochtendromerij –
Zelfs Het met
    vliegensvlug gevoel
        voor humor werd
                onmondig!

Kalend van de wereld drijven
zonder feestkilo's
    mijn levensavond tegemoet?

In Almere Muziekwijk stapte je uit

Maar niet voorgoed zag ik je
in het voorjaar weer
    onder het publiek
    van een talkshow

PALPITATIONS

You
   blond
      limpid and succinct
              little face
lea
   leafing
      adolescing

through a GQ-style magazine

smiled at me
five or
   so times

For all the swarms of Speech
   that beset me
      – my polar expedition dreams –
Even the One with
   the lightning sense
      of humour was
         rendered speechless!

Must I drift balding from the world
without a few party pounds
   towards the evening of my life?

You got out in Almere, Music District

But not for good I saw you
again that spring
   in the audience
   at a talk show

Treinnimf
    schrijf je mijn hachje?
Ik kan goed koken

Train nymph
    will you write my salvation?
I'm a good cook.

EENZAAMHEID RUIKT NAAR KALFSLEVER IN EEN OVENSCHAAL

Eenzaamheid ruikt naar kalfslever in een ovenschaal
de geur plakt in elke hoek van het huis
sneeuw en hoge bomen bakenen wegen af
Je komt niet weg voordat alles ontdooit
daarom trouwt men hier snel

Soms hakt er iemand een wak in het ijs
om te kijken of hij nog leeft
in de sauna worden vriendschappen geruild voor bier
Woorden zijn spaarzaam als het licht
als iemand wat vraagt
plak ik de mijne onder de sneeuw

In de keuken drink ik de laatste slokken
uit wijnglazen die op de afwas wachten
gekookte varkenshoofden gapen me aan
sneeuw wordt van daken geveegd

Ik verstop mij in een lichte roes onder het tafelkleed
pulk de inhoud uit een broodje
kijk waar muren elkaar raken

Loneliness Smells Of Calf's Liver In A Baking Dish

Loneliness smells of calf's liver in a baking dish
the smell sticks to every corner of the house
snow and tall trees mark off roads
You can't get away before everything thaws
that's why people get married quickly here

Sometimes someone hacks a hole in the ice
to see if he's still alive
in the sauna friendships are exchanged for beer
Words are as scarce as the light
when anyone asks anything
I stick mine under the snow

In the kitchen I drink the last dregs
in the wine glasses waiting to be washed up
boiled pig's heads gape at me
snow is swept off roofs

I hide slightly tipsy under the table-cloth
pick the innards out of a roll
look at where the walls touch each other

271

De Laatste Onbekende

Dus u heeft in het geheim geleefd, werd ondergronds
geboren, u bent nooit in beeld geweest.

Dus u woonde op plaatsen waar geen kijkers kwamen,
geen hond verlaten rondliep, neus dicht bij de grond,
u kwam nooit in verleiding iemand
duidelijk zichtbaar te aaien.

U nam geen goedgeschreven woorden in de mond,
had geen zorgvuldig gezicht – hoe,
als wij u niet zagen heeft u geleefd?

Hield u zich ergens voor iemand verstopt?
Leek het voor u andersom – raakten wij weg
zolang u geen deel had aan ons?

U kunt niet meer weggaan zoals u hier kwam,
in het donker, als een geheim. Blijft u
zo zitten dan zoomen wij in.

Dit is uw kans om aanwezig te zijn.

ESTER NAOMI PERQUIN 1980–

THE LAST UNKNOWN PERSON

So you've lived in secret, were born
underground, have never been in the picture.

So you lived in places where no one came to look,
no dog roamed desolately, nose close to the ground,
you were never tempted to
stroke anyone in full view.

You didn't utter any well-turned phrases,
didn't show a careful face – how,
if we didn't see you, did you live?

Were you hiding from someone somewhere?
Did you see it the other way round – did we vanish
as long as you had no part in us?

You can't leave the way you arrived,
in the dark, as a secret. Sit as
you are, and we will zoom in.

This is your chance to be present.

Oerknal

's Avonds zegt een natuurkundige op televisie
dat het ook mogelijk is dat het heelal op een dag
niet langer zal groeien, maar langzaam, sneller
dan het licht, ineen zal klappen. In dat geval
zouden er na ons nog triljoenen heelallen
kunnen ontstaan en hangen we nu slechts
onder aan een stamboom van universa. Stel je voor
dat je jezelf enkel voort kunt planten
door niet meer te bestaan.

's Ochtends, wanneer ik bij de start
van een dag zie hoe ik opnieuw ben gaan
ademhalen, vergelijk ik dit heen en weer
gegooi van sterren met mijn op en neer
gaande borsten, met de antenne van
een radio, die je doelloos in en uit
kunt blijven schuiven en vervolgens,
vooralsnog mijn meest geslaagde poging,
met een zeeanemoon.

Big Bang

One night on TV a physicist says
it's not impossible the universe will one day
stop growing and slowly, faster
than light, implode. In that case
trillions of cosmoses might succeed
ours and we'd now be left dangling
from a family tree of universes. Imagine
only being able to reproduce
by ceasing to exist.

Next morning, when at the
start of a day I see I've begun
breathing again, I compare this tossing
around of stars to the bobbing about
of my breasts, to a radio
aerial you can keep sliding aimlessly in and out
and then, my most successful shot to date,
to a sea anemone.

The landscape of Dutch poetry bears few resemblances to the terrain of the Low Countries as it is charted in the work of some of the best Dutch poets. Typically, the country one finds described in their work is monotonous, flat and desolate. It is the landscape we find in 'Memory of Holland', written by the expressionist author Hendrik Marsman (1899-1940). Written in 1936, after Marsman had moved to the Belgian town of Schaerbeek, 'Memory of Holland' is a well-known poem. It has become a vital part of the Dutch literary heritage: most readers know its lines by heart and in 2000 it was awarded the title of Best Dutch Poem of the Century. In Marsman's poem, however, Holland is not unequivocally valued: it is remembered as a country of 'infinite plains', scattered villages with 'truncated towers', where the sun is 'slowly stifled and greyed' by 'mist of all colours' and where the threatening 'voice of the water / with its endless disasters / is feared and obeyed'. The terrain of Holland, in other words, is metaphorically shaped by its backbreaking history and cramped mentality: it is the result of centuries of hard labour, dominated by a Spartan work ethic, and an on-going battle against water. These images of the landscape of the Netherlands and its connection to the Dutch character have their roots in a clichéd and debatable view of culture and society at large, but they continue to circulate in the cultural, social and political domain, shaping and disseminating the self-image of the Netherlands.

When we venture deeper into the history of Dutch poetry, however, other, more inviting and temperate landscapes are unfolded. This collection, in which the poetry from the Low Countries has been anthologized in an exemplary manner, allows us to become familiar with those other sides of Dutch-language literature. In it, we are first introduced, by an anonymous poet, to a landscape born of mild springs, where birds are a-nesting. Later we move to the mild countryside of the farmer-poet A.C.W. Staring (1767-1840), in which a swallow slips across the meadows, and plies 'over the sleek grass'; and on to the musical world of the Flemish priest Guido Gezelle (1830-1899), where Beethoven's Septet echoes in the movements of 'a little leaf' floating on a stream, where it 'skittle-scuttled just / like watter / and theer it ripple-ruffled just / like watter'. Travelling onwards, we encounter the swirling stream of Dutch Romanticism, for example in the work of Hélène Swarth (1859-1941) and Willem Kloos (1859-1936), or the still, but deep-running waters of symbolist poetry from P.C. Boutens (1870-1943) and Albert Verwey (1865-1937). The terrain changes and is expanded on, too. In the 1950s, for example, a group of poets labelling themselves the 'Movement of the Fifties' – including Lucebert (1924-1994), Gerrit Kouwenaar (1923-2014), Paul Rodenko (1920-1976), and Remco Campert (1929-), amongst others – started to write poetry inspired by Surrealism and Dadaism. Their joint literary efforts soon branched out and created a delta of experimental poetry, where 'simplicity's luminous waters' are expressed in 'poetic ways' (Lucebert) and in which the crashing surf 'regroups and so becomes poetry' (Campert). The ground keeps shifting and the terrain is continuously reorganized – as in, for instance, the poetry of K. Michel (1958-), who magically transforms the Royal Pond in The Hague, next to the seat of the States General of the Netherlands, into the sea itself, that 'silver-grey / that shimmering foaming, churning vast thing / that stretches there to the horizon beyond'. These poems offer the reader views of a diverse landscape, at times wild or even exotic.

These poetic vistas of the Netherlands, either off-putting or appealing, reveal something fundamental: a deep-rooted love-hate relationship between Dutch poets and their country. Dutch poetry, even though it springs from a culture famous for negotiation and compromise, reveals two extreme, incompatible views with regards to the self-image of the Netherlands. A middle ground seems non-existent: the country and its landscape are either admired or loathed. This introduction entails a closer inspection of this vexed self-image as we find it expressed in the anthologized poems; as such, this essay presents a topography of Dutch poetry that, I hope, may function as a travel guide, of use for both the readers who are exploring the literature of The Low Countries for the first time and those that are re-familiarizing themselves with it.

What is it, then, that makes some Dutch poets loathe their country, and why is its landscape the target of their critique? Marsman's 'Memory of Holland' already points in the direction of answers to these questions, but other telling examples are easy to find. 'Boutade' by P.A. de Génestet (1829-1861) is a case in point. De Génestet was an Amsterdam-born Remonstrant preacher with a passionate interest in literature. Inspired by Romantics such as Lord Byron or Alfred de Musset, De Génestet wanted to devote his life to poetry and greatness. Sadly, De Génestet succumbed to tuberculosis in 1861, but we can still find traces of his Romantic nature in his bitter complaint 'Boutade'. In this poem, he addresses his fatherland, ironically referred to as 'ancestral ground most holy', with the following lines: 'Oh land of filth and fog, of vile rain chill and stinging, / a sodden fetid plot of vapours dank and damp, / a vast expanse of mire and blocked roads clogged and clinging, / brimful of gamps and gout, of toothache and of cramp!' De Génestet's critique is harsh as it stands, yet it reveals itself as even harsher when one takes into account that he wrote his poem in a time when nationalism and patriotism were on the rise. All over Europe romantic authors were making a case for the love of the fatherland, the intimate relation between a nation's *Boden* and the poet's *Blut*, and, consequently, between the soil of a country and the language of its authors. De Génestet's poem goes against the grain, then, but in another sense it is representative of a traditional complaint directed at the Netherlands. The focal point of his lament is the Dutch landscape, which is depicted as a 'dreary mushy swamp', filled with 'marsh frogs, dredgers' and 'mud gods overrun', as De Génestet writes. According to the classical theory of the four humours, that underlies this complaint's logic, these environmental conditions have a detrimental effect on the Dutch temperament. De Génestet writes: 'To mud your claggy climate makes my blood set slowly / song, hunger, joy and peace are all withheld from me.' The frustrated poet, wishing he were more like a hot-blooded Romantic or a great poet filled with melancholy, thus presents himself as the flegmatic, 'besnotted son' of the Dutch climate.

In hindsight, it is tempting to dismiss De Génestet's comments as historically bound, as a typical, albeit recalcitrant, example of nineteenth-century cultural determinism, along the lines of Hippolyte Taine's theory on the importance of 'race, milieu et moment' for a nation's literature. Yet such a dismissal would be to ignore that the supposed connection between a country's climate and soil on the one hand and a culture's qualities on the other hand is part and parcel of an influential tradition that has outlived nineteenth-century romanticism and nationalism. This tradition, in fact, continues to inform the representation of Dutch culture. De Génestet's 'Boutade' may date from 1851, but the same logic is at work in Marsman's 'Memory of Holland' from 1936, as quoted above: the poet provides the 'voice of the water' with words and foregrounds its impact on the nation's mentality. This logic, in a very literal sense, is a topographical one: the place or region (*topos*) writes itself (*graphia*) onto the character of the poet and from there into his culture.

This tradition of a topographical mapping of a landscape onto its culture ties in with – and elaborates on – a common-place view on the Netherlands. According to this view, it is a country oppressed by wind and rain, thwarted by Protestant religion, and further crushed by an all-embracing bureaucracy. It is not surprising, therefore, that Dutch language and history are rich with topographical metaphors denoting one form of critique or another. In the last decades of the eighteenth century, for example, the phrase 'Holland at its most narrow' ('Holland op z'n smalst') took root. At first, the phrase used to refer to the part of the province North Holland situated between the North Sea and the IJ, a mere seven kilometres wide. The Protestant minister Nicolaas Beets, who served as unappointed poet laureate of the Netherlands during the nineteenth century, praised this part of the Netherlands in his 1860 poem 'Cutting Through Holland at its Most Narrow' ('Doorgraving van Holland op zijn smalst'), written on the occasion of the digging of the North Sea Canal. Soon, however, the phrase took on a very different meaning. In 1873, the lawyer and politician Victor de Stuers (1843-1916) published an article bearing the title 'Holland op zijn smalst' in the influential literary journal *De Gids*; in it, De Stuers criticized the government for its failing policy regarding the preservation of Dutch cultural heritage. Ever since, 'Holland at its most narrow' has become a popular shorthand for a form of pettiness or narrow-mindedness (specifically with regard to Dutch culture and tradition), which is believed to be typical of the society of the Netherlands in general.

The logic of topography is reaffirmed by more recent discussion on the state of Dutch literature. The narrowness of the Netherlands (and thus, supposedly, of its people) is an often-used rhetorical motive in the public forming of opinion on literature and culture. It is not uncommon in public debates that participants take the position that the Netherlands has always been 'too narrow' for its own canonical authors. This argument appeals to the fact that important figures such as Multatuli (1820-1887), author of *Max Havelaar* (1860), W.F. Hermans (1921-1995), one of the great post-war novelists, or Gerrit Komrij (1944-2012), poet laureate of the Netherlands from 2000-2004, preferred to live abroad. In fact, in 1982 Komrij published his own take on Marsman's 'Memory of Holland', affirming the image of the Netherlands as a country stifled by religion and bureaucracy. His version of the opening of the poem reads: 'Thinking of Holland / I see security bonds / pass through greedy fingers / lines of Batavians / lusting for merchandise / standing on the pulpit / like prunes.'

Finally, it is telling that the connection between the landscape of the Netherlands and its mentality has not only influenced public discussion about Dutch literature, but political discourse as well. A famous aspect of the Dutch political system, after all, is also framed in topographical terms: the 'Polder model', denoting a traditional form of public deliberation that allows citizens, unions and the state to negotiate about wages, working conditions and governmental policy. Advocates of this model often present it as an example of a political win-win situation, the result of an open dialogue and successfully form of institutionalized democracy. Opponents, however, explore the less rosy connotations of the image of the polder and stress its negative aspects: in their eyes, the model leads to the marshlands of compromising, a wholesale levelling of income, and a watering-down of policy. The logic of topography, in other words, continues to shape political thought.

What we find, then, is a pattern in which loathing of (or at least a harsh critique) of one's culture is framed as a loathing of that country's landscape and climate, and vice versa. This pattern points to a deep-rooted tendency of the Dutch to look down upon their cultural heritage. This tendency, as we will see, is only half of the story, but its influence is undeniable: studies in cultural self-representation and national stereotypes confirm that the Dutch self-image is characterized by a relativistic and anti-authoritarian stance. The cultural legacy of the Netherlands is all but immune to this relativism; in fact, at times it seems as if the Dutch take pride in putting their own artistic efforts in critical perspective. Paradoxically, those cultural figures who engage in a sharp critique of Dutch culture are often valued most highly. In the light of this, it is revealing that that there is a common Dutch word for patriotism or love of the fatherland, 'vaderlandsliefde', but no prevalent antonym. From the examples above, however, it becomes clear that some Dutch poems give voice to a form of 'vaderlandshaat', hatred of one's fatherland: or, to use a technical term, misopatriotism.

Nonetheless, there is another side to the Dutch self-image. It is the face of a country that is not as desolate and marshy as some poets may suggest. We find richer, more diverse landscapes, as suggested above, in the work of Staring, Gezelle or Michel. Another fine example is 'Holland' by E.J. Potgieter (1808-1875). Potgieter was a sharp critic and an esteemed spokesman. His poem 'Holland' chimes with De Génestet's complaint about his home country. Along the lines of his fellow-poet, Potgieter addresses 'Holland' directly: 'Grey are your heavens and stormy your strand / bare are your dunes and dead-flat your acres, / Nature employed here a stepmother's hand', he writes. Yet then he takes a different turn: 'All that you are our fore-fathers have made; / from a morass the toil of those makers, / who resisted both sea and tyranny's blade, / built a temple to Freedom and true Faith displayed.' As in De Génestet's poem, the landscape is seen as the fruit of hard labour, wrought from the sea, but this time with a difference: for Potgieter, the nation's soil provides a firm ground for 'true order's shrine', a 'refuge of those oppressed by harsh power'. Of course, one could question to what extent the 'refuge' of Potgieter, who had the reputation of a harsh critic, is accessible for those not adhering to the 'true Faith', but even so: with this poem, we move into a space that is not by definition oppressive or narrow. 'Holland' becomes an open, inviting space and a trustworthy foundation. A comparable scenario is presented in a poem by Willem Bilderdijk, spiritual leader of the Dutch counterpart of the *Réveil* movement and one of the greatest Romantics known to the Netherlands. In 1795, Bilderdijk was banned from the newly established Batavian Republic, because he refused to acknowledge its authority. Upon his return to his country of origin in 1806, he composed the poem 'On Holland's Shore', in which he relates to his readers the experience of stepping 'from the flood that round me swept / onto Holland's solid shore'. Instead of sinking into De Génestet's 'dreary mushy swamp' and breathing its 'vapours dank and damp', Bilderdijk finds solid footing and fresh air. He rests his limbs on 'its earth' and inhales 'its air's sweet charm'. Intriguingly, this other perspective on the Dutch self-image invokes the same topographical logic that we found at work in misopatriotic poetry. The details of landscape and climate have remained the same, yet the outcome of the process is the complete opposite: the 'infinite plains', as Marsman would say, now provide a solid foundation for order, while the stormy skies ensure the supply of fresh air, both in a literal and a figural sense.

Some Dutch poets push this logic even further and maintain that a drab environment and a narrow-minded mentality are conditions that the Dutch should appreciate and cherish.

This argument is elaborated in the poem 'The Dapperstraat' by J.C. Bloem (1887-1966). Characterized by critics as the poet of eternally unfulfilled desire, Bloem rose to fame with aptly titled collections such as *Defeat* (*Nederlaag*, 1937) and *Quiet Though Sad* (1946), remaining influential until well into the 1960s. 'The Dapperstraat' can easily compete with Marsman's 'Memory of Holland' for the title of best know Dutch poem. In it, the poet paints a picture of a rather unimpressive country: 'nature' is reduced to 'a stretch of woodland, postage stamp in size, / a hill with some small houses on the side'. Like De Génestet, Bloem describes a country with a 'drab and drizzly' climate. Yet in Bloem's poem, the clouded skies and the narrow perspective turn out to be essential: they provide the poet with aesthetic bliss and the experience of happiness. After all, 'when, skylight-framed, [the clouds] all go drifting past', he reflects, their 'beauty cannot be outdone'. A limited perspective, in other words, brings out the best in life, for: 'Life hides its miracles till, without warning, / They're suddenly displayed in all their art.' It is this insight that leaves the poet 'downright happy', while he is drenched by rain, one morning in the Dapperstraat. Of course, Bloem was a poet who regularly played up his romantic tendencies for the sake of effect: as a result, it is possible to read 'The Dapperstraat' as an ironic, implicit critique of a 'skylight-framed' view of life. Such a reading becomes even more tempting when one takes into consideration that the Dutch word 'domweg' ('downright') can also be translated as 'foolishly'. Nonetheless, Bloem's repeated praise for the beauty of the Netherlands (in other poems he writes about 'the misunderstood beauty of the landscape of Holland' and 'Holland's pale and fragile spring sun') suggests his appreciation for its topography was, at the very least, an element of his authorial image that was intentionally repeated and that we need to take seriously.

Of course, one can object to these interpretations that authors such as Potgieter, Bilderdijk or Bloem might put a more positive spin on the logic of topography, but that they do not depict an altogether different landscape of the Netherlands. A possible

explanation could be that misopatriotism is simply an inaliena-
ble trait of the Dutch: in that case, Marsman was right all along.
Yet a closer inspection of the reception of Dutch poetry teaches
one that the literature and culture of the Netherlands do have
the potential for a topographical remapping and a shift away
from misopatriotism. It is revealing, for example, that especial-
ly the opening lines of Marsman's famous 'Memory of Holland'
are continuously rewritten by Dutch readers, for a wide variety
of reasons. Examples are abound. On a website about sustain-
able entrepreneurship: 'Thinking of Holland I see black terns,
gracefully traversing infinite plains.' A governmental folder on
town and country planning: 'Thinking of Holland I see rivers
flowing through climate-robust plains.' The title of a successful
scientific research proposal: 'Thinking of Holland I see churn-
ing rivers.' On the online historical portal of the Dutch Public
Broadcasting System NPO: 'Thinking of Holland I see wind-
mills, fishermen, small bridges and a little pub at the harbour.'
One individual, contributing to the lyrics of the 'King's Song'
composed by the public, on the occasion of the coronation of
the present King Willem-Alexander in 2013, suggests as a
line: 'Thinking of Holland I see the King diligently visiting
cities and villages; he fights for the rights and wishes of all his
people.' And finally, in a nationally broadcasted 2011 television
commercial for the Dutch newspaper *De Telegraaf*, a voice-
over rewrote the first lines of Marsman's poem as: 'Thinking of
Holland / I see the land of plover's eggs / a first day of spring,
of cleaning the house / the winter coat, back into storage again
/ heating's on, heating's off / where we run outside en masse /
at the first sight of a sunbeam.' These alternative versions of
'Memory of Holland', improvised as they may be, suggest new
topographies – new connections between the landscape and the
mentality of its inhabitants.

Finally, contemporary poets and artists, too, engage in
such a fundamental revision of Dutch topography. Doing so,
they make clear that redrawing the borders of the terrain does
not imply a return to old-fashioned patriotism or nationalism.
Sensing the effects of globalization, immigration, cultural,

political and economic changes, they present us with a new and extremely changeable version of the Netherlands, tracing the contours of its hopes, its ambitions, and its internal tensions. Ramsey Nasr (1974-) provides us with a fascinating example of this development. Nasr is a poet, opinion maker and actor who embodies Dutch culture in post-nationalist times: born of mixed descent, part Palestinian and part Dutch, he became city poet of the Belgian city of Antwerp in 2005; three years later, he was chosen as poet laureate of the Netherlands. In his work, he investigates the extremes and paradoxes of Dutch culture. The poem 'In the Land of Kings' from 2009 is a merciless reflection on the contemporary Netherlands. 'I live in a land', Nasr writes, 'where the animal-lover decides / from sheer goodness to shoot a fellow human // I live in a land / where the righteous believer decides / from respect to plant the knife in the heretic.' The landscape is no longer determined by geographical details (nor by outdated topographical clichés), but by the behaviour and choices of its inhabitants. For those familiar with recent Dutch history, the references are clear: the first stanza refers to the murder of the populist politician Pim Fortuyn (1948-2002) by the environmentalist Volkert van der Graaf (1969-), the second to the slaying of the director and columnist Theo van Gogh (1957-2004) by the religious extremist Mohammed Bouyeri (1978-). With these references, Nasr highlights events that have had a profound impact on Dutch society. The poem goes on to conclude that the Netherlands has become a 'red, red twilight land / where boundaries have been totally erased / where responsibility's professed ad nauseam / where sixteen millions kings have been raised'. In this poem, Nasr offers us a bleak and cynical perspective on the current state of affairs in the Netherlands.

Fortunately, contemporary Dutch culture provides us with alternative scenarios. Nasr's poem, in fact, seems to engage in a dialogue with the 2005 number one hit song 'The land of' ('Het land van') by hiphop artists Lange Frans and Baas B. The first line of their song mirrors Nasr's poem: 'I'm from the land of Pim Fortuyn and Volkert van der G./ the land of Theo van Gogh and

Mohammed B.' Like Nasr, Lange Frans and Klaas B. question the nation's cultural climate, where 'one is cut down at the moment when one is about to make it', where 'stinginess' prevails, and *Apartheid* is 'the most famous word from Dutch language'. Yet at the same time, they appeal to the cherished diversity and openness of Dutch society: they emphasize that they share their country with 'Turkish, Moroccan and Surinamese' inhabitants. It may be, they conclude, that the Netherlands is 'ticking like a time bomb', but it is country that they have 'locked in their hearts' nonetheless. For better or for worse, then, the stifling mists and the dreary landscape of the Netherlands are replaced by artists like Nasr or Lange Frans and Baas B by a country where the grounds are continuously debated and boundaries are being rene-gotiated, with uncertain results. It is this topographical dynamic that provides an endless source of inspiration for Dutch poets – and an invitation to their readers to explore the new terrains they discover.

Gaston Franssen, Amsterdam
January 2015

SOURCE OF ORIGINAL POEMS

Poems 1 to 36, and 41 to 43 are in the public domain. The source text can be found in various publications, but we especially recommend the Digitale bibliotheek voor de Nederlandse letteren (Digital Library of Dutch Literature) http://dbnl.org/ and the Komrij anthologies:

De Nederlandse poëzie van de 12de tot en met de 16de eeuw in 1000 en enige bladzijden, ed. Gerrit Komrij, published by Bert Bakker, 1994
De Nederlandse poëzie van de 17de en 18de eeuw in 1000 en enige gedichten, ed. Gerrit Komrij, published by Bert Bakker, 1986
De Nederlandse poëzie van de 19de en 20ste eeuw in 1000 en enige gedichten, ed. Gerrit Komrij, published by Bert Bakker, 1980.

37 Willem Elsschot, 'Het Huwelijk', *Verzen,* Manteau, 1934
38 Jacques Bloem, 'De Dapperstraat', *Verzamelde gedichten,* Athenaeum, 1968
39 P.N. van Eyck, 'De tuinman en de dood', *Verzamelde gedichten,* Van Oorschot, 1958-1964
40 Martinus Nijhoff, 'De moeder de vrouw', *Verzameld werk,* Bert Bakker, 2001
44 Jan Engelman, 'Vera Janacopoulos', *Sine nomine,* De Gemeenschap, 1930
45 Gerrit Achterberg, 'Jachtopziener', *Verzamelde gedichten,* Querido, 1964
46 Ida Gerhardt, 'Het carillon', *Verzamelde gedichten,* Athenaeum, 1980
47 M. Vasalis (ps. M. Drooglever Fortuyn-Leenmans), 'De idioot in het bad', *Verzameld werk,* Van Oorschot, 1999
48 Jan Hanlo, 'Niet ongelijk', *Verzamelde gedichten,* Van Oorschot, 1970
49 Leo Vroman, 'Bloemen', *262 gedichten,* Querido, 1974

67 Jules Deelder, 'Blues on Tuesday,' *Renaissance: gedichten '44-'94*, De Bezige Bij, 1994

68 Anna Enquist (ps. C. Widlund-Broer), 'Verzoek aan de schilder', *Gedichten 1991-2012*, De Arbeiderspers, 2013

69 Frank Koenegracht, 'Nazomer', *Dichters van deze tijd. De Nederlandstalige poëzie na 1960,* Gent: Poëziecentrum, 1994

70 Hester Knibbe, 'De rivier', *Een dunne duurzaamheid*, Prometheus, 1999

71 Leonard Nolens, 'Zeg aan de kinderen', *Manieren van leven. Gedichten 1975-2011*, Querido, 2012

72 Anneke Brassinga, 'Tot God', *Timiditeiten*, De Bezige Bij, 2003

73 Eva Gerlach, 'Solve et coagula', *Een bed van mensen vlees,* De Arbeiderspers, 2003

74 Martin Reints, 'Oud vergaderzaaltje', *Lopende zaken*, De Bezige Bij, 2010

75 Stefan Hertmans, 'Marsyas', *Muziek voor de overtocht. Gedichten 1975-2005*, De Bezige Bij, 2005

76 Willem Jan Otten, 'Op de hoge', *Op de hoge*, Van Oorschot, 2003

77 Joke van Leeuwen, 'Er woonde op de aarde'. *Ozo Heppiejer*, Querido, 2000

78 Tonnus Oosterhoff, 'Een goed mens is iets heel eenvoudigs', *Wij zagen ons in een kleine groep mensen veranderen,* De Bezige Bij, 2002

79 Arjen Duinker, 'XXIV', *Losse gedichten*, Meulenhoff, 1990

80 Esther Jansma, 'Bodemonderzoek', *Voor altijd ergens*, Prometheus, 2015

81 K. Michel, 'Ook de vissen', *Kleur de schaduwen*, Augustus, 2004

82 Anne Vegter, 'Showen en trippen', *Spamfighter,* Querido, 2007

83 Erik Menkveld, 'De nieuwe vis', *Prime Time,* Van Oorschot, 2005

PUBLISHER'S ACKNOWLEDGEMENTS

The publisher has attemped, within reason, to contact all copy-right holders and thanks them for their permission to translate and reprint the original texts.

Detailed acknowledgements for each poem are printed in the SOURCES OF ORIGINAL POEMS section.

PAUL VINCENT

Paul received a BA (Hons) Modern Languages (German, Dutch, French) from University of Cambridge, UK in 1964. He undertook Postgraduate study at the University of Amsterdam during 1965-1966. He was awarded an MA from University of Cambridge in 1968.

From 1967 to 1989 he was a full time Lecturer and Senior Lecturer in Dutch Language and Literature at Bedford College, University of London, and afterwards at University College London. He left his academic career in 1989 to become a freelance translator of Dutch and German into English.

He has translated many of the leading authors and poets from the Low Countries including Louis Couperus, Harry Mulisch, Willem Elsschot, Louis Paul Boon and Hugo Claus.

He was the recipient of the first David Reid Poetry Translation Prize for the translation of Hendrik Marsman's famous poem 'Herinnering aan Holland' (Memory of Holland) in 2006, awarded by the Foundation for the Production and Translation of Dutch Literature.

In 2012 Paul Vincent received the Vondel Prize for *My Little War*, his translation of *Mijn kleine oorlog* by Louis Paul Boon, published by Dalkey Archive.

Paul Vincent is based in London.

Holland Park Press is a unique publishing initiative. It gives contemporary Dutch writers the opportunity to be published in Dutch and English. We also publish new works written in English and translations of classic Dutch novels.

Visit www.hollandparkpress.co.uk for more information, and to visit our bookshop http://hollandparkpress.co.uk/books.php

You can also follow us in the social media:

http://www.twitter.com/HollandParkPres
http://www.facebook.com/HollandParkPress
http://www.linkedin.com/company/holland-park-press
http://www.youtube.com/user/HollandParkPress

Printed in the USA/Agawam, MA
November 5, 2015

625865.001